ENDORSEMENTS

"This book is a robust and accessible critique of Modern Monetary Theory, and is a must-read for anyone looking to equip themselves for the next frontier of popular economic debate."

Harvey Nriapia, *Financial Times*

"A sharp, critical, and highly entertaining introduction to the debates surrounding Modern Monetary Theory. Maggiori draws from ill-fated monetary experiments all around the world—including his own experience growing up in Argentina—to illustrate the questions that MMT advocates still have to answer."

William Quinn, author of *Boom and Bust: A Global History of Financial Bubbles*

"An excellent critique of MMT. Emmanuel Maggiori is a patient and affable guide to this strange branch of economics and offers some useful insights from real economics along the way."

Dr. Christopher Snowdon, Institute of Economic Affairs

"MMT sounds like a magic fix, but this book reveals why it's an economic ticking time bomb. If you care about the future of our financial system, you need to read this before it's too late."

Jesse Wright, Host of *El Podcast*

IF YOU CAN JUST PRINT MONEY, WHY DO I PAY TAXES?

IF YOU CAN JUST PRINT MONEY, WHY DO I PAY TAXES?

MODERN MONETARY THEORY DISTILLED AND DEBUNKED IN PLAIN ENGLISH

EMMANUEL MAGGIORI

WILEY

This edition first published 2026
© 2026 by John Wiley & Sons Ltd

All rights reserved, including rights for text and data mining and training of artificial intelligence technologies or similar technologies. No part of this publication may be reproduced, stored in a retrieval system, or transmitted, in any form or by any means, electronic, mechanical, photocopying, recording or otherwise, except as permitted by law. Advice on how to obtain permission to reuse material from this title is available at http://www.wiley.com/go/permissions.

The right of Emmanuel Maggiori to be identified as the author of this work has been asserted in accordance with law.

Registered Offices

John Wiley & Sons, Inc., 111 River Street, Hoboken, NJ 07030, USA
John Wiley & Sons Ltd, New Era House, 8 Oldlands Way, Bognor Regis, West Sussex, PO22 9NQ, UK

For details of our global editorial offices, customer services, and more information about Wiley products visit us at www.wiley.com.

The manufacturer's authorized representative according to the EU General Product Safety Regulation is Wiley-VCH GmbH, Boschstr. 12, 69469 Weinheim, Germany, e-mail: Product_Safety@wiley.com.

Wiley also publishes its books in a variety of electronic formats and by print-on-demand. Some content that appears in standard print versions of this book may not be available in other formats.

Trademarks: Wiley and the Wiley logo are trademarks or registered trademarks of John Wiley & Sons, Inc. and/or its affiliates in the United States and other countries and may not be used without written permission. All other trademarks are the property of their respective owners. John Wiley & Sons, Inc. is not associated with any product or vendor mentioned in this book.

Limit of Liability/Disclaimer of Warranty: While the publisher and the authors have used their best efforts in preparing this work, including a review of the content of the work, neither the publisher nor the authors make any representations or warranties with respect to the accuracy or completeness of the contents of this work and specifically disclaim all warranties, including without limitation any implied warranties of merchantability or fitness for a particular purpose. No warranty may be created or extended by sales representatives, written sales materials or promotional statements for this work. The fact that an organization, website, or product is referred to in this work as a citation and/or potential source of further information does not mean that the publisher and authors endorse the information or services the organization, website, or product may provide or recommendations it may make. This work is sold with the understanding that the publisher is not engaged in rendering professional services. The advice and strategies contained herein may not be suitable for your situation. You should consult with a specialist where appropriate. Further, readers should be aware that websites listed in this work may have changed or disappeared between when this work was written and when it is read. Neither the publisher nor authors shall be liable for any loss of profit or any other commercial damages, including but not limited to special, incidental, consequential, or other damages.

Library of Congress Cataloging-in-Publication Data has been applied for:

ISBN 9781394375257 (Hardback)

ISBN 9781394375271 (ePub)

ISBN 9781394375318 (ePDF)

Cover Design: Wiley
Cover Image: © Ruslan Lytvyn/Getty Images

Set in 11/16pt Minion Pro by Lumina Datamatics

SKY10149544_031426

CONTENTS

INTRODUCTION — 1

CHAPTER 1
THE MODERN MONETARY THEORY WORLD — 13

CHAPTER 2
THE REAL WORLD — 41

CHAPTER 3
QUANTITATIVE EASING — 61

CHAPTER 4
INFLATION — 79

CHAPTER 5
UNEMPLOYMENT, AND HOW TO FIX IT — 115

CHAPTER 6
HOW TO SAVE THE PLANET AND INCREASE PROSPERITY — 135

CONCLUDING REMARKS: MMT AND THE FUTURE OF ECONOMICS — 153

CONTENTS

APPENDIX A
   MMT ON BITCOIN   163

APPENDIX B
   MORE MMT RED HERRINGS   167

APPENDIX C
   MMT ON QUANTITATIVE EASING   179

APPENDIX D
   MORE ON INFLATION   181

ACKNOWLEDGMENTS   185
ABOUT THE AUTHOR   187
NOTES   189
INDEX   211

INTRODUCTION

A couple of years ago, I went out for dinner with my extended family. At the end of the meal, we agreed to split the bill. The waitress told us the card reader wasn't working, so we had to pay cash. Chaos ensued.

My aunt opened her handbag, took out a thick wad of cash, and spread it out on the table. My other aunt took out several rolls of banknotes, which she'd organized using elastic bands. My cousin took a thick wad of cash from an outsized wallet.

In a few seconds, the table became filled with *hundreds* of banknotes. The waitress used a machine to count them.

This was during a trip back to my hometown in Argentina. While this looked like a scene taken from a mafia movie, it was business as usual. This was an ordinary meal at an ordinary restaurant.

Argentina was experiencing high inflation, which meant prices were going up and up very rapidly. Existing banknotes—even the highest valued ones—couldn't cope with the much-increased prices, so people had to carry stacks of them to pay for basic stuff.

The scene at the restaurant took me by surprise. I grew up in Argentina and experienced inflation firsthand. But, after I moved out of the country in 2014, inflation accelerated significantly. On every subsequent visit to

INTRODUCTION

Argentina, I found the situation more and more striking. Between my last two trips, which were two years apart, prices were multiplied by a factor of eight.

Argentina has suffered from repeated bouts of high inflation throughout its history. Every once in a while, the central bank replaces the existing currency with a new one with zeros removed, which makes it more readable. Think of replacing "dollars" with a new currency called "bollars" and declaring one bollar worth one billion of the old dollars. Since the 1970s, Argentina has removed 13 zeros from its currency.

The traditional explanation for this phenomenon is that, instead of raising taxes or borrowing money, the Argentine government often creates new money to pay for its spending. This creates an excess of money—there's more money going around than people want—so money loses its value, and prices go up.[1]

This view is so universally accepted that most people think it's a bad idea to let the government create money to pay for its spending. So, they think this practice must be prohibited. The government is thus forced to be disciplined and "balance the books"—if it wants to spend one dollar, it must first obtain one dollar through taxes. The government can also borrow money from the private sector, but it must do so sparingly because taxes may have to be increased in the future to repay the debt. This can burden future generations.

But what if this isn't how things work? What if, with the right precautions, money creation could be used by the government as a force for good? What if we were missing out on good stuff by *not* letting the government create money and spend it more freely?

Since the mid-1990s, a group of economists have been saying just that. They think the government could use its power to create money to accomplish new things and tackle some of society's greatest challenges. It could, for example, eliminate unemployment, increase prosperity, and protect the planet. If done correctly, this practice would have no adverse consequences, such as inflation. Our obsession with balancing the books is thus holding us back, as it restrains government spending in an unnecessary way.

These economists put their thoughts together into a theory. They called it *Modern Monetary Theory*, or just *MMT*.

Nobody took them seriously. In the beginning, most people thought MMT didn't say anything useful and would be a recipe for Argentina-style debacle. So, it remained confined to fringe academic circles.

But things have changed. The theory has been gaining prominence and making its way into the public eye. Some people praise it, and others bash it.

Just to cite a few examples, in 2019, Nobel Prize winner Robert J. Shiller wrote a *New York Times* article entitled, "Modern Monetary Theory makes sense, up to a point."[2] That same year, Jerome Powell, the chairman of the US Federal Reserve, dismissed the theory in front of the US Senate, calling it "just wrong."[3]

A year later, Mervyn King, the former governor of the Bank of England, published an article on the *Spectator* called, "The ideological bankruptcy of Modern Monetary Theory."[4]

In 2021, the *Wall Street Journal* published an article entitled, "Modern Monetary Theory isn't the future. It's here now."[5] In 2024, the same newspaper wrote, "Modern Monetary Theory has never worked."[6]

MMT has been endorsed by some politicians, including Alexandra Ocasio-Cortez and Bernie Sanders.[7] The latter hired Stephanie Kelton, a prominent MMT proponent, as his chief economic advisor during his presidential campaign.

In 2020, Kelton published a book called *The Deficit Myth*, which became an instant *New York Times* bestseller. The book promotes MMT in an accessible manner, and it's helped bring MMT to the attention of the general public.

MMT has become too big to ignore, so it is now mentioned in the newest editions of popular economics textbooks.[8]

There were at least three major events which propelled interest in MMT. Let me briefly discuss them in chronological order.

First, economists failed to predict the 2008 financial crisis. This generated distrust in mainstream economics and fostered interest in alternative, or "heterodox," economic theories. MMT is one of the most prominent contenders.

Second, central banks around the world responded to the 2008 crisis by using unprecedented and unconventional policies. One of them, called *quantitative easing*, involved creating a huge amount of money—out of thin air—to try to reactivate the economy. Many people have compared quantitative easing with MMT.[9]

Third, the response to the COVID-19 pandemic reminded a lot of people of MMT, which caused an explosion of interest in the theory. Notably, central banks around the world created a huge amount of money—again, out of thin air—to help stimulate the economy during the pandemic. Many people think this money was directly used to help fund governments' generous stimulus packages, which included things like handing out checks to households and paying the wages of private-sector employees.

But if this was possible during the pandemic, why not do it all the time? Perhaps MMT had been right all along—we can indeed achieve new things by letting the government create money and spend it more freely.

According to a *New York Times* article, MMT went through a "victory lap" during the pandemic. The title of the article was, "Is this what winning looks like?"[10]

In 2020, MMT proponent Randall Wray said:

Barely twenty years later, MMT had achieved something quite rare for heterodox economics: it was in the headlines all over the world—and in quick succession first denounced by all respectable policymakers, politicians, and economists and then suddenly embraced as the necessary response to a global pandemic.[11]

But not so fast! Inflation surged around the world in 2021. In many countries, it rose to the highest level in decades. The United States, for example, experienced its highest inflation in nearly 40 years. Policymakers quickly said it was caused by pandemic-related supply chain disruption and, later on, due to the war in Ukraine. But many people remained unconvinced. They thought the remarkable money creation which took place during the pandemic had something to do with it. Perhaps MMT's victory lap had been premature.

MMT concerns us all because, if it keeps gaining popularity, it could guide future policymakers. If MMT is right, this is good news—MMT will help us live in a fairer, safer, and greener society. If not, it could lead to Argentina-style inflation.

So, is MMT the key to prosperity or a recipe for disaster? This book will help you find out.

THE THREE PRINCIPLES OF MMT

I think MMT can be organized into three main principles. These principles will guide us throughout the remainder of this book. Let's briefly go through each of them in an informal way.

Principle 1: The Government Could Stop Worrying About Money

We often hear that the government is running out of money, that it can't afford carrying out a certain project, that its debt will be a burden to future generations, and so on.

MMT says that, if the government is in full control of its own currency, like in the United States, the United Kingdom, and Japan, then these worries are unnecessary. This is because the government—at least hypothetically—could pay for stuff by creating new money.

One consequence of this is that the government doesn't really *need* your taxes to be able to afford stuff. The government could create money instead. This doesn't mean taxes can be eliminated. MMT says taxes are still needed for other reasons, which we will discuss later, but they're not essential to let the government pay for stuff.

Another consequence is that government "debt" is not really debt in the usual sense. This is because the government could choose to pay it off in a jiffy by creating new money. As a result, we shouldn't consider government debt a burden.

MMT says that restrictions on government spending are "self-imposed." For example, if a government is *not* allowed to spend above a certain amount, this is a voluntary choice and not the result of an absolute impossibility for the government to spend more, as it could create money if it wanted to. Similarly, if a government is not allowed to "borrow" above a certain threshold, this is a voluntary choice and not the result of debt being a genuine burden.

This doesn't mean there are no limits to what the government can do. For example, it can't build a road if there are no available machines, labor, and materials to do so. If the government doesn't recognize these technical limits and still tries to build an impossible road, the result is inflation. So, while governments need not worry about things like "debt" or "running out of money," they should worry about spending too much on the wrong things, as it could cause inflation.

MMT's conclusion is that, when politicians worry about government finances, their worries are either unwarranted or a phony, politically motivated charade. They're self-inflicted and unnecessary pain. It is possible at any point to remove self-imposed restrictions and let the government spend more freely, letting it create money if needed.

Principle 2: The Government Already Creates New Money Daily to Pay for Stuff

The previous principle was hypothetical—it said governments "could" create money to pay for stuff if they wanted to. But do governments do this in the real world?

MMT says that, contrary to popular belief, governments already create a lot of money *routinely* to pay for stuff. In fact, this is how the US federal government usually pays for things. For example, when the US Department of Defense buys a fighter jet, the government creates new money—out of thin air—to pay for it.

Most people think the government fills up its bank accounts with tax money, and then it spends that money. MMT says this is wrong. This mistaken view arises from an incorrect analysis of the nitty-gritty accounting details. MMT fixes these accounting errors.

MMT has dedicated a lot of effort to proving this principle. But why does it matter so much? By developing this point, MMT tries to show us how much of a ridiculous charade it is to say things like "the government is running out of money" or "the government can't afford this or that." The United States and many other countries are already creating money routinely, so why pretend otherwise?

Principle 3: If We Loosen Restrictions on Government Spending, We'll Increase Prosperity

Imagine we removed restrictions on government spending, such as budgetary limits, debt ceilings, and so on. We could let the government spend more freely and create money as needed to pay for it.

MMT says that, if this power is used carefully, it will enable the government to do more things without adverse consequences. For example, it is possible for the government to reduce unemployment without causing an increase in inflation and without negatively affecting the private sector. So, there are "free lunches" that the government could exploit. Policymakers haven't exploited these opportunities yet due to their unnecessary self-imposed restrictions. Removing the shackles unlocks a world of new possibilities.

This is the principle that makes MMT truly interesting because it impacts policymaking and has the potential to generate genuine gains for society. If the government follows MMT's guidance, it could increase prosperity in a way it currently cannot.

THE PEOPLE OF MMT

Before we start, let me briefly introduce you to the people behind MMT. We'll call them *MMTers* throughout this book.

The MMT debate was launched by financier Warren Mosler. In 1996, he circulated an article on the internet that laid out the foundations of MMT.[12]

His ideas were noticed and further developed by a group of heterodox economists. Three of them are particularly noteworthy because they're prolific authors of MMT articles, blogs, and books. These are Stephanie Kelton, William Mitchell, and Randall Wray. I will be quoting them a lot all over this book.

Almost every MMTer has been at some point affiliated with the University of Missouri–Kansas City. This is the most important MMT think tank. For example, Kelton and Wray worked together there. Financier Warren Mosler has provided donations to support research at this institution.[13]

In addition, almost every MMTer has collaborated with the Levy Economics Institute, a public policy think tank based in Annandale-on-Hudson, New York.

When they're not hanging out at the University of Missouri or at the Levy Institute, MMTers tend to work as economics professors at lesser-known universities and liberal arts colleges, such as Lewis & Clark College, Franklin & Marshall College, and Wartburg College. MMTers tend to be based in the United States, with a notable exception being William Mitchell, who is in Australia.

Let me also introduce you to the two new stars of the show: Éric Tymoigne and Yeva Nersisyan. They both joined the MMT movement later than the others, but they soon become their most fervent and prolific defenders. They're both alumni of the University of Missouri–Kansas City. I'll be quoting them a lot too.

Finally, an honorary mention goes to MMTers Mathew Forstater, Scott Fullwiler, and Pavlina Tcherneva. They're mostly known for their work on the job guarantee program, which is MMT's flagship policy. They've all been affiliated to the University of Missouri–Kansas City at some point.

Throughout this book, you'll also hear from Brett Fiebiger, Thomas Palley, and Marc Lavoie. These are MMT's most prominent critics. As opposed to shallower critics, these have taken the time to read MMT in detail and question it in an informed way. Such is the case that MMTers have publicly replied to their criticism. Fiebiger and Palley work as independent economic advisors, and Lavoie is an economics professor at the University of Ottawa.

These three critics have one thing in common: They think the government should have a larger role in stimulating the economy. So, they sympathize with MMT's ultimate political goal: bigger government. However, they don't think MMT is the correct compass to get there.

INTRODUCTION

WHY I'M WRITING THIS BOOK

I like to get to the bottom of things. The more difficult this is, the more fun I have doing it. As I started hearing more about MMT, I decided to dive into it.

I soon realized that getting to the bottom of MMT was quite challenging. The academic work by MMTers is long and messy. It often uses words in a nonstandard way and goes off on tangents. In addition, MMTers have written articles to respond to criticism, then the critics responded to these responses, and then MMTers responded to the responses to the responses.

To top it off, nonacademic work, such as the book *The Deficit Myth*, doesn't help much, as it's extremely lopsided in favor of MMT—it contains untruths and doesn't address criticism.

I realized the world was missing an easy-to-read, comprehensive account of MMT. I took up the challenge myself. I've studied economics, I have an academic and mathematical background, and I like to write books that demystify stuff. So, I thought I was a suitable candidate for it. I read more than 3,000 pages of MMT work—both by its proponents and its critics—and organized the material and translated it into simple terms.

The book you're reading is the result. I hope you'll find it insightful and fun.

HOW THIS BOOK IS ORGANIZED

Chapter 1, called *The Modern Monetary Theory World*, discusses a hypothetical world proposed by MMT. In this world, the government creates new money whenever it spends. This addresses MMT's first principle, which, if you remember, says that the government could stop worrying about money.

Chapter 2, called *The Real World*, studies the second principle, which says that current, real-life governments already create new money when they spend. This, if true, makes the real world much closer to the MMT world than we think.

Chapter 3, called *Quantitative Easing*, comments on whether recent policies may have made the real world more MMT-like. This concludes our analysis of the second principle.

For the rest of the book, we study the third principle, which says that loosening government spending restrictions could be used as a force for good.

Chapter 4, called *Inflation*, describes MMT's explanation of why inflation happens and how to fight it. It also covers MMT's explanation of hyperinflation, such as the one experienced in Zimbabwe in the 2000s.

Chapter 5, called *Unemployment, and How to Fix It*, tells us MMT's explanation of what causes unemployment. It also proposes a solution: the government must offer a guaranteed job to anyone who needs one.

Chapter 6, called *How to Save the Planet and Increase Prosperity*, covers other policies proposed by MMT.

CHAPTER ONE

THE MODERN MONETARY THEORY WORLD

At the height of his career, Nicolas Cage was one of Hollywood's highest paid actors—he once made $40 million in a single year. He also had very expensive tastes. He bought 13 houses, two private islands, a private jet, and two castles in Europe, although he never even stayed in one of those castles. In one year alone, Cage bought 22 cars, including nine Rolls-Royces.[1] He also paid $276,000 for a dinosaur skull.[2]

Cage soon found himself on the verge of bankruptcy—he'd depleted his bank accounts and taken on too much debt. In 2009, he couldn't afford to pay an income tax bill and started facing legal issues. Some of his properties were seized and auctioned away by the banks. He reportedly started "taking roles left and right to help pay off his debts."[3] Notably, he took roles in 29 quickly produced, low-budget movies that were never screened in cinemas.

Regardless of your income, you need to be careful about your spending. All households—yours, mine, and Nicolas Cage's—are financially constrained. This means you must make sure to spend less than you bring in. Otherwise, you'll soon find yourself in trouble. Even if banks may help you out—through credit and loans—they won't do so forever.

We tend to think of the government in a similar way. Just like a household, the government must collect enough income—in the form of taxes—to pay its bills. If it doesn't, it risks running out of money. If the government spends more than it collects, it must borrow money from the private sector to bridge the gap. However, many people are afraid that too much borrowing will burden future generations with higher taxes. Moreover, if a deeply indebted government fails to pay its debts, which is known as a *default*, its credit score will go down, and it will find it harder and more expensive to borrow money in the future.

Governments run their budgets like households, so they try to contain their spending and limit their borrowing. For example, the US government sets a limit to the amount of money it can borrow, and the EU imposes a similar restriction to its member countries.

The household view of the government is espoused by politicians all over the political spectrum. During a speech, senator and future president Barack Obama explained:

> The fact that we are here today to debate raising America's debt limit is a sign of leadership failure. It is a sign that the US government can't pay its own bills. It is a sign that we now depend on ongoing financial assistance from foreign countries to finance our government's reckless fiscal policies.[4]

At a conservative conference, Argentine economist and future president Javier Milei explained:

> The problem with government debt is that it's future taxes, which means the cost of partying hard by current generations is passed on

to our children, grandchildren, and people who haven't even been born yet, let alone voted. In fact, one of the things I've proposed in Argentina is that, in order to make childbirth less traumatic, instead of giving babies a spank we should tell them how much money they owe—this will make them cry like crazy![5]

The household view is also echoed by the media. A *New York Times* article explains:

> The so-called X-date is the moment when the United States is unable to pay its bills, including interest payments to investors who hold government debt. Failure to meet those obligations could result in the United States defaulting on its debt. The U.S. has never defaulted on its debt.

Modern Monetary Theory—from now on we'll call it MMT—does not agree. In fact, MMT says the household view is the *worst* way to analyze the economy of the United States and of many other countries. MMT proponent Stephanie Kelton tells us, "Don't think of a household" and adds:

> If you've heard someone complain that Washington needs to get its fiscal house in order, you've heard a version of the household myth. It derives from the flawed idea that we should look at Uncle Sam's budget through the same lens we use to manage our own family budgets.[6]

MMT focuses on countries that have their own currencies, like the United States and the United Kingdom. In these countries, the government could technically create as much money as needed to pay for stuff and repay its debts. So, they don't have money problems or financial restrictions. According to MMT, this makes them very different from households.

MMT proposes an alternative way of understanding the economy, in which the government is nothing like a household. Stephanie Kelton says, "What if I could convince you that we can have an economy that puts people and planet first? That finding the money to do this is not a problem? ... Another kind of society is possible, one in which we can afford to invest in healthcare, education, and resilient infrastructure."[7]

This chapter explains MMT's proposed way to model and understand the economy. We will call it the *MMT world*. I'll add caveats to supplement and question the model as we go. We'll also analyze the model's relation to many topics, such as the value of money, the role of taxes, and the meaning of government debt.

I must warn you about something though. The MMT world is an imaginary world—it is a very simple, hypothetical model of an economy, and it does not necessarily correspond to reality. MMT proponents argue that, despite its simplicity, the MMT world is still the most useful and accurate way of thinking about most economies. They often say we should analyze policies *through the lens of MMT* instead of through the lens of a household. Very often, MMTers speak of current governments, such as the United Kingdom and the United States, as if they already operated just like in the MMT world, thus putting the hypothetical model and the real world in the same bag. This has made readers confused and frustrated.

So, to make things easier, in this chapter we won't focus on the real world. Instead, we will analyze the fascinating hypothetical MMT world and the conclusions we can draw from it. I ask you to suspend disbelief for now. We will discuss MMT's relation to the real world later on. Let's get started!

THE ESSENCE OF MMT

Imagine that the government wants to build a bridge. After receiving quotes from multiple suppliers, it picks a firm called Smith Engineering. The firm quotes $10 million for the job.

In the MMT world, the government has a peculiar way of paying for stuff—it just creates new money out of thin air. In this example, the government creates a new $10 million and deposits it in Smith Engineering's bank account. In this world, the government just spends money into existence.

This is technically very easy to do in the modern era because most money is digital, which means that bank account balances are just numbers inside computers. You can think of it as a long Excel file that says who has how much:

Account Holder	Balance
Paul Jones	$1,400
Jane Doe	$35
Smith Engineering	$50,000

In order to pay Smith Engineering, all the government must do is replace the relevant number with a higher number inside the computer:

Account Holder	Balance
Paul Jones	$1,400
Jane Doe	$35
Smith Engineering	~~$50,000~~ $10,050,000

The engineering firm now sees a higher balance in its account, which it can use as it wishes. In practice, this may require a few coordinated operations between the government and banks, but the details are not necessary to understand MMT.

The government also has a peculiar way of receiving payments, such as taxes and fines. Suppose Smith Engineering must pay a $2 million tax bill to the government. When the firm transfers the money to the government, the latter simply makes that amount disappear from the record. For this, the government just replaces the relevant number with a lower number inside a computer:

Account Holder	Balance
Paul Jones	$1,400
Jane Doe	$35
Smith Engineering & Co.	~~$50,000~~ ~~$10,050,000~~ $8,050,000

Note that the government doesn't even need to have a bank account with a certain balance recorded in it. Instead, whenever it spends, it creates new money, which increases the total amount of money in others' bank accounts. When it collects taxes or other payments, it destroys money, which reduces the total amount of money in others' bank accounts. The government faces no technical impediments to do this.

This process is very different from how the rest of us spend. Regular folks don't have the power to create or destroy money, which would be a lot of fun. When we spend, we move money across accounts, but the total amount of money remains unchanged:

Account Holder	Balance
Paul Smith	~~$1,400~~ $1,000
Jane Doe	~~$35~~ $435
Smith Engineering & Co.	$8,050,000

Note that, in the MMT world, the government may not necessarily create the same amount of money that it destroys. If the government spends more money than it destroys, it increases the total amount of money in the hands of the public. This money can then be used by the public for private payments, so it can circulate around the economy. Conversely, if the government creates less money than it destroys, it decreases the total amount of money in the hands of the public.

This is the essence of MMT. It can be summarized using the following statement: The central government spends and receives payments by creating and destroying money.

While this may seem very simple at first, it can be a useful tool to analyze a model economy, and, as we'll see throughout the rest of this chapter, it provides some fascinating answers to many questions.

But there's a catch: the MMT world cannot possibly function in *any* country. There are a few conditions. Let's quickly go through them.

THE THREE CONDITIONS OF MMT

There are at least three important conditions to make the MMT world possible. First, the country must be *monetarily sovereign*. This means that it must issue its own national currency. A country like Ecuador, which uses US dollars instead of having its own currency, cannot operate the MMT way. This is because it doesn't have the power to edit the computers that keep track of dollar balances, which are controlled by the United States. Later in the book, we'll talk more about Ecuador and why it uses US dollars.

A second condition for MMT is that the country must use *fiat* currency, which means the government doesn't promise to exchange it against anything else, such as gold. This was the case for a long time in history—central banks stored gold in their vaults, and people could turn up and ask to exchange their banknotes for physical gold. This isn't admitted in the MMT world. This is because such a promise prevents the government from creating money freely, as the amount of money must be matched by a sufficient amount of gold stored in its vaults.

The third condition is that the country must have a *floating exchange rate*, which means the government does not promise a predetermined, guaranteed exchange rate against a foreign currency. Otherwise, it faces the same problem as with gold—it needs to keep enough foreign currency in its vaults to be able to fulfill its promises. Countries like Jordan and the UAE, which offer a guaranteed exchange rate of their national currencies against the US dollar, cannot operate the MMT way.

MMT also assumes that only the highest level of government, usually known as the central or federal government, has the power to create and destroy money. Regional and local governments, such as the city of New York, are not allowed to do that. So, lower-level governments are akin to households—they must think carefully about their budgets and can find themselves in Nicolas Cage–style situations.

One final remark is that there is no central bank in the MMT world. We usually think of the central bank, such as the US Federal Reserve ("the Fed") or the Bank of England, as the entity in charge of creating, destroying, and managing the national currency. In the MMT model, there is none.

MMT doesn't say that a central bank cannot exist. However, it is pointless to study it separately because the government can create and destroy money freely. So, the central bank would be under full control of the government—it would be a government department like any other. MMT absorbs the central bank as part of "the government."[8]

We can summarize the conditions of MMT into the following statement: *The national currency has zero strings attached.* In other words, there are no promises to convert it to gold, foreign currency, or anything else. This way, there are no technical restrictions that would impede the central government to create and destroy money.

We're now ready to use the MMT lens to answer all sorts of important questions. Why are taxes needed? Is debt a burden? Does the government face any limits? Let's go!

TAXES DRIVE MONEY

In 1690, the government of the Massachusetts Bay Colony found itself in quite a pickle. After trying and failing to occupy Quebec, the returning troops—who were starving and plagued with smallpox—wanted to be paid. But the government was completely broke. At that time, payments were usually made using tangible goods like precious metals, grains, and land, but the Massachusetts government had very little of that to offer. Its coffers were empty of precious metals, and the government had already committed future grain stocks to settle other debts. Moreover, the colony's existing land belonged to the King of England and not to the colony's administration, so it couldn't be offered for payments.[9]

The government had no choice but to pay the troops and other suppliers by issuing pieces of paper, which they called *bills*. These pieces of paper were stamped and signed by the authorities, and they contained a written monetary value, such as "twenty shillings."[10]

The government could not make any credible promises to exchange such bills for silver, grains, land, or anything else. So, its bills weren't "backed" by anything—they were flimsy pieces of paper that couldn't be exchanged against tangible stuff.

The challenge was to make people accept those bills for payments. Imagine I offered to buy your car in exchange for a napkin on which I wrote the words "ten thousand dollars." Would you give me your car? At first sight, the Massachusetts bills weren't much better than that.

The government had to get creative to have its bills accepted. So, it came up with a clever idea: It announced that the public could use these bills for future tax payments. In fact, taxpayers would get a 5% discount on their taxes if they paid using those bills instead of the usual grains. So, the bills were not that flimsy after all—they were useful to pay taxes. The government promised that, once it recuperated its own bills through tax payments, it would destroy them. It once publicly burned the bills after tax collection to reassure the public about its commitment to this operation.

At first, people were a bit skeptical about the bills. However, they soon started accepting them as payments from the government, as they knew they could use them to pay future taxes. People soon started using the bills to buy stuff from one another in private transactions, replacing old forms of money like grains and silver. So, these apparently flimsy bills become the colony's currency of choice for most transactions.

Let's travel back to the present day. The MMT world is a modern version of the Massachusetts colony—the government creates new money when it spends and destroys it when it collects taxes. Instead of printing and burning pieces of paper, it does so in a digital way, but the principle is the same.

MMT says that, in the world of MMT, the reason people accept payments in the government's digital money is the same as in Massachusetts—it's taxes. The government imposes taxes on individuals and businesses, and it only accepts its own digital money for tax payments. This creates a demand for the government's money, as people must obtain it to pay taxes. Smith Engineering is willing to build a bridge for the government in exchange for its newly created money because it knows it will need that money later to pay taxes—or someone else will.

In the MMT world, you may not be able to convert the government's digital money into gold, but you can convert it into the privilege of not finding yourself in court for failing to pay your tax bill. So, MMTers often say that *taxes drive money*.[11] They say there may exist other reasons why people accept the government's money, but taxes are *sufficient* for it.[12]

There's a meme circulating around the internet that says, "If you can just print money, why do I pay taxes?" MMT has an answer to that—taxes are a tool to guarantee that the money "printed" by the government is accepted by the public.

Note that, in the MMT world, taxes are not *needed* to fund the government because the government just creates new money whenever it spends. From a logical point of view, government spending comes first, during which new money is created, and taxation comes second, during which the previously created money is taxed out of existence.

ARE TAXES ENOUGH THOUGH?

During a recent trip to Argentina, I walked by a store that sold secondhand computers. I noticed their prices were all quoted in US dollars instead of the local currency—the Argentine *peso*.

At the time of my trip, Argentina had been suffering from years of rampant inflation. This meant that prices had been going up and up over time, or equivalently, the peso had become increasingly less valuable, as one peso could buy you less stuff over time. In the year preceding my trip, for example, inflation had been around 200%, which meant prices had more than tripled.[13] Or, equivalently, the peso had lost so much value that by the end the year you could buy three times less stuff with one peso than in the beginning of the year.

The owner of the computer store must have gotten tired of updating and updating price labels. So, he went for US dollars instead, whose value tends to be much more stable over time.

The prevalence of inflation contributes to Argentineans' recurring use of dollars to quote prices. Argentineans constantly mix pesos and dollars when they talk about prices. The higher the stakes, the least Argentineans use pesos. For example, house prices are only quoted in US dollars. If you tell an Argentinean how much you paid for your house in pesos, they will mentally convert it to dollars to understand what you mean.

If you go to mercadolibre.com.ar, the Argentinean version of eBay, you'll see cars are sometimes quoted in pesos and sometimes in US dollars. On a quick browse, I just saw a Toyota Hilux going for 18,000 US dollars next to a Chevrolet Onix going for 24,999,500 Argentine pesos. Living in Argentina requires doing some interesting mental gymnastics.

Argentineans often use US cash to buy stuff from one another, and dollar bills circulate widely around the economy. In fact, you can *only* buy a house using US cash. One of my Argentinean friends once escorted another friend to the real estate agency to help him feel safer, as he was carrying a bag with 50,000 US dollars in cash to buy an apartment. This was a legit transaction, and neither of my friends was a drug lord.

A website that helps foreigners buy property in Argentina explains:

> Most transactions are conducted using cash, primarily in the form of US $100 bills. It sounds primitive but this is how it is ... If you plan to make a purchase, you should prepare for the need to transport a substantial amount of US dollar bills into the country—potentially as much as $250,000 ... You will be required to provide a justification for the source of the money to AFIP [the tax bureau] through a local accountant. UIF [which investigates money laundering] will almost always request information.[14]

Inflation is a major contributor to this phenomenon. As a house seller, would you want to receive a large sum of pesos, whose value may drop dramatically before you even have time to spend it?

Argentineans never save money using pesos. Due to inflation, this would be like saving in icicles and putting them out on the balcony in the middle of the summer. If an Argentinean finds themselves with spare pesos, they will immediately try to exchange them to protect their savings. Most commonly, they will exchange them for US dollars, but they may also buy other currencies or even stuff, like a fridge.

At the time of my trip there, it was illegal to buy foreign currency except in very limited circumstances. So, Argentineans routinely exchanged their spare pesos for dollars in the black market. The black market was extremely well developed and completely overt. On a walk around downtown Buenos Aires, you were offered many chances to exchange currency in the black market. Black-market exchange rates were announced on every news program on TV under the name "blue dollars."

Economists consider something to be *money* if it fulfills three main roles. First, it should be a *unit of account*, which means a standard unit used to price things. The Argentine peso fulfills this role in a mediocre way, as people often price things using US dollars instead.

The second role of money is to be a *medium of exchange*, which means buyers and sellers use it as a token to facilitate trade. The Argentine peso also performs this role poorly. Notably, you can't buy a house using pesos.

The third role of money is to be a *store of value*, which means that people keep it as savings for future consumption. The Argentine peso fails spectacularly at this role.

So, while the peso may be Argentina's national currency, it's not quite what we usually understand by money.

This story tells us that the MMT mantra "taxes drive money" should be taken with a grain of salt. Argentineans pay taxes using pesos. However, pesos fall short of being a proper form of money.

In the MMT world, the best-case scenario is that the government's currency becomes widely accepted as a unit of account, medium of exchange, and store of value. In the worst-case scenario, people may only want the government's currency for the bare minimum. Perhaps they'll only want it to pay taxes—because they must—and they will flee the currency for anything else.

A better mantra might be "taxes drive the money needed to pay taxes." The acceptance of government currency beyond taxes is not guaranteed. This can complicate things a little for MMT. For example, if the government wants to spend more money than it collects from taxes, it might struggle to get its money accepted.

MMT doesn't tell us much about which conditions, other than taxes, may be necessary to guarantee that the government's currency is *widely* accepted by the public. To MMTers, it all seems to come down to taxes. MMT proponent Randall Wray explains:

> The situation can be very different in developing nations ... The tax liability can be limited by tax avoidance and evasion ... With a foreign currency used in private payments, and with widespread tax avoidance and evasion, the population might not want much of the government's own currency.[15]

Wray doesn't explain why in these countries people use foreign currency for private payments in the first place. He doesn't explain either if there's a minimum level of tax to make sure that "taxes drive money" in a wider sense. For example, if taxes are 30% of GDP, is that enough to have properly functioning money that fulfills all its roles? Or should taxes be, say, 40%? MMT doesn't explain this.

MMT proponent Éric Tymoigne adds that, if people don't widely adopt the national currency, it is because they don't trust "the government's ability and willingness to impose and enforce tax."[16] He says this can happen due to "wars, political instabilities, technical problems, errors in setting up a monetary system, and ignorance."[17]

MMT critic Marc Lavoie is not convinced. He says, "MMT authors often claim that a currency has value only because it must be used to pay taxes ... but this seems to overly minimize the importance and role of confidence and credibility for the worth of a currency."[18]

I'm not entirely convinced by MMT's story either. It seems to me that the government's currency must fulfill other requirements to become widely accepted and turn into properly functioning money. At the bare minimum, it must have a more-or-less stable value. Otherwise, people will run away from it—just ask an Argentinean.

OTHER ROLES OF TAXES

In the MMT world, taxes drive money. There are, however, at least three other uses of taxes. Let's quickly review them.

First, taxes can be used for redistribution of income. If we think in terms of "stuff" instead of money, which many economists like to do, we can interpret income as the right to obtain a portion of the goods and services produced in the economy every year, such as a mattress, a holiday, or a doctor's consultation. A person's income determines the share of that production they can buy—a higher earner can buy higher-quality mattresses, go on longer holidays, and access exclusive healthcare. The allocation of income is not always seen as fair. The role of taxes is to redistribute it, transferring it from the richer to the poorer, so that lower earners end up accessing a higher proportion of the production than they would otherwise. MMT proponent Stephanie Kelton says, "We can, and must, tax the rich. But not because we can't afford to do anything without them."[19]

Second, taxes are a tool to fight inflation. MMT says that, in some rare circumstances, a surge of spending in the economy can cause prices to go up because people bid increasingly more on products and services. A surge of spending could come from the private sector. For example, companies may become optimistic about a new technology and invest in it. It could also come from the public sector. For example, the government may embark upon an epic infrastructure project. An increase in taxes can be used to discourage private spending and thus reduce outbidding to keep inflation under control. Stephanie Kelton explains:

> If the government wants to boost spending on healthcare and education, it *may* need to remove some spending power from the rest of us to prevent its own more general outlays to push up prices. One way to do this is by coordinating higher government spending with higher taxes so that the rest of us are forced to cut back a little to create room for additional government spending.[20]

Remember that, according to MMT, such a tax increase is not a way to "pay" for healthcare and education, as the government can spend money into existence. A tax increase is just a tool that may *optionally* be used if such spending risks causing inflation. We shall have a lot to say about MMT's understanding of inflation later on.

The final role of taxes is to encourage or discourage certain behaviors. Examples of this are cigarette taxes and tax abatements for electric vehicles.

To summarize, taxes have four functions:

- Make people accept the government's currency for payments.
- Redistribute income.
- Reduce consumption to fight inflation, if necessary.
- Deter undesirable behaviors and promote desirable ones.

Note that funding the government does not appear in this list. The government spends money into existence, so taxes aren't needed to fund its spending in any way.

Let's now move on to some of MMT's most remarkable conclusions, which have been widely publicized in books, blogs, and newspapers.

THE GOVERNMENT CANNOT RUN OUT OF MONEY

MMTer Randall Wray explains, "Government cannot run out of money; it can always financially afford to take care of our own."[21] MMTer Stephanie Kelton adds, "There is absolutely no good reason for Social Security benefits, for example, to ever face cuts. Our government will always be able to meet future obligations because it can never run out of money."[22]

The idea that the government cannot run out of money is one of the most publicized corollaries of MMT. Sometimes it's explained using more technical words, such as, "the government has no hard financial constraints," but it means essentially the same thing—that the government doesn't have money problems. MMTers have called this "one of the main contributions of MMT."[23]

There are two things I'd like to point out about this. First, it is true that, in the MMT world, the central government cannot run out of money. Second, such an observation isn't particularly insightful—if a government can create as much money as it wants, then *evidently* it cannot run out of it. When MMTers say that the government cannot run out of money, they assume that the government operates the MMT way—it is allowed to spend money into existence. So, it automatically follows that it cannot run out of money. This "main contribution" of MMT is a truism because it simply restates MMT's assumptions using different words.

It is well understood that a government cannot run out of money *if it is allowed to create it*. Most economists don't like the idea of giving the government the power to create money because they're afraid of the consequences, not because they think it's technically impossible. MMT critic Thomas Palley says, "The critical question is not whether government can finance spending without taxes. Everybody knows it can [by creating money]. Instead, the question is what are the macroeconomic consequences of doing so and should the government do so?"[24]

Imagine we gave Nicolas Cage the possibility of spending money into existence. Can we trust him not to engage in indiscriminate spending and cause a mess? Perhaps he'd try to buy the entire Santa Monica coastline, which will increase property prices in Santa Monica for everyone else and affect related markets, such as construction and decorating. Economists don't want governments to be allowed to spend money into existence for the same reasons they don't want Nicolas Cage to be allowed to do so.

Note that, in the MMT world, local and regional governments operate just like a household—they cannot create and destroy money. But why stop MMT at the central government? Why not also let the government of New York City or even Nicolas Cage spend money into existence? MMT's implicit assumption is that the central government can be trusted to use that power in a benevolent and safe way while others cannot.

GOVERNMENT DEBT ISN'T DEBT

Every week, the US government conducts an auction where the public can give it money in exchange for a certificate that says, "I owe you." The certificate stipulates a schedule in which the government pays the bearer their money back, plus interests. For example, you give $100 to the government, and the certificate says you will receive $100 ten years later plus $5 every year until then. This certificate is known as a *government bond*.

We typically say that the government *borrows* when it issues or "sells" a bond, and we describe outstanding government bonds as the *national debt*. When the government wants to spend more money than it collects from taxes, it borrows money from the public to cover the difference, and it does so by issuing bonds.

Let's now travel to the MMT world. Is there a place for bonds in this world, given that the government can create money and thus doesn't need to borrow? Surprisingly, MMT says, "Yes." However, we should not think of bonds as "debt" or "borrowing."

In the MMT world, bonds are just an alternative form of government money. The difference with ordinary money is that bonds pay the holder an interest over time. Stephanie Kelton calls ordinary money "green dollars," and she calls bonds, which are just interest-bearing money, "yellow dollars."

When the government "borrows" money, all it does is remove some "green dollars" from the economy and replace them with "yellow dollars." For example, if the government "borrows" $100 from the private sector, it withdraws $100 green dollars and replaces them with a $100 bond. Stephanie Kelton explains, "What we call government borrowing is nothing more than Uncle Sam allowing people to transform green dollars into interest-bearing yellow dollars."[25]

The government voluntarily chooses to perform this "swap" if it thinks it's a good idea to help people collect interest. This decision is voluntary. Stephanie Kelton says, "Why does the government need to borrow? The answer is, it doesn't. It *chooses* to offer people a different kind of government money, one that pays a bit of interest."[26]

Let me add a few comments to this. First, it is true that, in the MMT world, the government doesn't need to "borrow" in the usual sense. Second, this isn't surprising. MMT assumes the government is allowed to create money whenever it wants, so it naturally follows that the government doesn't need to "borrow" and that bonds aren't really "debt." This is a direct conclusion of MMT's assumptions. Once again, MMT offers a truism rather than an interesting insight.

Finally, I'm not sure I'd describe bonds as a different type of "money." This is because bonds are usually not used for payments. When was the last time you paid for your groceries using a government bond?

Unlike a $100 bill, which is worth exactly $100 now, a bond says, "I'll pay you $100 in ten years." As a result of impatience and uncertainty, people won't accept bonds at face value in the present. Instead, a bond that promises $100 in the future may be resold in the present for, say, $80, and this value may change quickly. This makes bonds difficult to use as money for ordinary transactions. So, it's a little too simplistic to declare bonds to be a type of money.

THE GOVERNMENT COULD PAY OFF ITS DEBT TOMORROW

Stephanie Kelton says, "The entire national debt could be paid off tomorrow, and none of us would have to chip in a dime."[27]

In the MMT world, because the government can create money, it can easily pay off any debt it owes in its own currency. So, MMT tells us not to worry about the government accumulating debt, as it can be wiped out through a few keystrokes. Kelton explains, "There is zero risk of the US being forced into default by its creditors. That's because the government can always meet its obligation to turn those yellow dollars into green dollars."[28]

While this is technically true, there is a major caveat. The government can still default on its debt but in a different way.

Suppose you buy a government bond for $100. The bond promises to pay you $100 back in 10 years plus an interest of $5 every year until then. Now, imagine the currency suffers from an unexpected bout of inflation over the next few years. As a result, you can afford less stuff with the $5 you receive every year, and the final $100 can't buy you nearly as much stuff as you had in mind. The government still defaults on its promise—as you're worse off than you thought—even if doesn't default on its payments.

So, in the MMT world, the government can still default *economically* even if it cannot default technically—all it takes is for the government's money to lose its value.

Let's go back to Kelton's comment, where she says, "… none of us would have to chip in a dime." Suppose the government creates a vast amount of money to pay off its debt in one go, thus replacing all outstanding bonds with money.

Most of these bonds were probably in the hands of money managers, such as pension funds. After the government replaces them with newly created, ordinary money, the fund managers will want to invest this money in something else, so they can generate returns for their clients. As government bonds are no longer an option, they'll find other ways to invest the money. They may, for example, lend the money to private companies. This would help these companies embark upon new projects. However, this could cause inflation because companies will bid up on products and services to run these new projects.

Perhaps the fund will invest some of the money in shares of Apple. This will increase the price of these shares and could make anyone who owns them feel richer. This could make people spend more and thus also bid up on products and services, causing inflation. This mechanism is called quantitative easing, and we'll have more to say about it later.

So, wiping out debt could cause inflation through different channels, which means money would lose its value and anybody with spare cash would end up worse off. This doesn't sound like the public "not chipping in a dime."

GOVERNMENT DEFICITS MAKE US RICHER

Let's go back to the Massachusetts colony of the late 1600s. If you remember, the colony operated in an MMT-style way by spending money into existence and taxing it out of existence. Initially, the plan was to destroy every shilling that was created, so the amount of tax would exactly match the amount of spending. However, people started complaining about the pressure of paying taxes and asked for relief. The government responded by repeatedly postponing the collection of taxes, so the government kept creating new money without retiring the money as initially intended. Historian Andrew McFarland Davis explains:

> In 1702, the practice was begun of postponing the time for levying the tax through which the bills should be called in. At first it was for one year. In 1704, the retirement of a part of the issues was carried forward to two years. In 1707, the time was lengthened to three years. In 1709, a part of the issues were not to be provided for until five years had elapsed. In 1711, the limit reached six years, and in 1714, another year was added. In this manner the dates for levying the taxes which were to retire the bills were from time to time postponed until 1722, when £6,000 were issued not to be called in for thirteen years. Then an effort was made to cure this evil, and for a brief time short periods were assigned for retirements. These, however, were again lengthened, until, in 1730, £13,000 were issued which were not to be called in until 1741.[29]

The Massachusetts government ran a deficit, which means it spent more money than it collected through taxes. When this happens in the MMT world, the public is left with increasingly more money in its hands, as more of it is created than destroyed.

According to MMT, this makes people richer, as they end up having increasingly more money. MMT proponent Éric Tymoigne explains, "Fiscal deficits are a boost to the saving level of the domestic private sector, state and local governments, and the rest of the world."[30]

MMTer Stephanie Kelton adds:

> Fiscal deficits don't eat up our savings; they enlarge them! ... *In purely financial terms*, every fiscal deficit is good for someone. That's because government deficits are always matched—penny for penny—by a financial surplus in the nongovernment bucket ... Fiscal deficits will *always* lift our collective (financial) boat.[31]

Kelton adds that this isn't an opinion; it's the cold hard reality of accounting.[32]

I will add two comments to this. First, it is indeed true that, in the MMT world, a government deficit leaves the public with more money in its hands. This is self-evident—if you create more money than you destroy, people will indeed have more money.

Second, there is a gigantic caveat. The new wealth in the hands of the public is *paper* wealth, not real wealth. Real wealth is made up of machines, factories, houses, and so on. These are capable of producing stuff. Paper wealth does not produce stuff—it is a promise that you'll be able to buy stuff with it in the future. In the case of Massachusetts, deficits literally put more pieces of paper in the hands of the public. In the modern MMT world, in which money is digital, deficits simply increase the total amount of money recorded inside banks' computers—think of marking up numbers on Excel spreadsheets.

Stephanie Kelton is careful enough to always add the qualifier "financial" when she says that deficits increase our savings. She says that deficits "lift our collective (financial) boat," that deficits make a "financial contribution" to the public,[33] and so on. The word financial means "paper."

The problem with paper wealth is that it can lose its value over time. An MMT-style government may offer the public a "financial contribution" of, say, $100, by running a $100 deficit. However, $100 may be worth much less in the future if the currency suffers from inflation.

This is exactly what happened in Massachusetts. The government kept spending bills into existence while refusing to collect as much in taxes, which put increasingly more bills in the hands of the public. However, the currency suffered from rampant inflation. Within a few years, the Massachusetts paper money lost most of its value. The public had more bills in its hands, but it didn't seem to be getting any richer.

Due to this remarkable inflation phenomenon, in 1751, the British prohibited the colony from creating anymore paper money, and the colony adopted silver coins as its primary currency. That was the end of Massachusetts' MMT experiment.

WHAT ARE THE LIMITS?

In the MMT world, the central government doesn't have an affordability problem, as it can create as much money as it wants. But surely it must face limits! There must be things money can't buy.

MMT says that the government is limited by the economy's technical capacity to produce stuff. For example, the government cannot build an entire hospital in one day, as this is just not technically possible. It can't either build 1,000 houses if there aren't enough materials or workers to build them. MMTer Randall Wray explains:

> Anything that is technologically feasible is financially affordable. It comes down to technology, resources, and political will. We've got the technology and the resources.[34]

MMTer Stephanie Kelton adds:

> Every economy has its own internal speed limit, regulated by the availability of our *real productive resources*—the state of technology and the quantity and quality of its land, workers, factories, machines, and other materials ... MMT is not about removing all limits. It's not a free lunch. It's about replacing our current approach, one obsessed with budget outcomes, with one that prioritizes human outcomes while at the same time recognizing and respecting our economy's real resource constraints.[35]

MMT says we should stop asking ourselves whether the government has or doesn't have the money to pay for something. Instead, we should ask ourselves whether the economy has the technical capacity to do the required work. Are there enough construction workers? Are there enough materials?[36]

MMTers believe that our economies usually have a lot of spare capacity. Stephanie Kelton says, "Peacetime economies never operate at full capacity. There is always slack in the form of unemployed resources, including labor."[37] MMTer Éric Tymoigne adds, "In most cases, economies have more flexibility than what is admitted."[38]

So, while limits do exist, MMTers think they're rarely reached. As a consequence, governments are missing out on the possibility of doing more stuff. MMTers describe this as available *policy space* that isn't fully exploited.

According to MMT, a government that can create money can better exploit the available policy space, as it doesn't have to worry about paying the bills. So, in the MMT world, the government can effectively mobilize spare resources to let the economy operate at full capacity. As a result, the government can conduct more public works, improve healthcare, reduce unemployment, and so on. This comes at no cost.

But what if the government tries to push the economy beyond its technical limits? What if it tries to, say, build a hospital when there are no more available construction workers and materials? According to MMT, the result is inflation. This is because, when companies don't have any more spare capacity to produce products, they start increasing prices.

Thus, the MMT recipe for policymaking is to increase government spending to try to push the economy very close to its maximum productive limits, but it shouldn't try to exceed those limits. *Voilà!*

All I'll add for now is that MMT's views on unemployment, inflation, and policymaking are quite naive. We'll get back to these topics in later chapters.

THE END OF SELF-FLAGELLATION

In February 2025, the Trump administration established the Department of Government Efficiency, or DOGE, whose goal was to cut down government spending. This was partly triggered by the mounting amount of government debt and the fact that interest payments had become the second highest government expense, only surpassed by Social Security.

In the mid of this debate, one of my LinkedIn contacts said, "Countries can't go bankrupt if they issue their own currency. Comparing sovereign debt to a household budget (or even a corporation), means you're either woefully uneducated or deliberately lying. And probably a sadist. You love the suffering, be honest."

This contact, who is well versed in MMT, describes worrying about government debt as an unnecessary act of self-flagellation.

I don't think this is coincidental. For a long time, MMTers have implied the same thing, although using softer words. Éric Tymoigne and Randall Wray explain:

> MMT recognizes that there are some self-imposed constraints on the financial operations of the government ... MMT insists there is nothing "natural" about the operating procedures (including restrictions).[39]

Stephanie Kelton adds:

> MMT recognizes the real limits from delusional and unnecessary self-imposed constraints.[40]

The MMT world is free from unnecessary shackles that limit the government.

Let me add two comments. First, it is well known that restrictions are self-imposed and could be removed. We could technically let local governments and even Nicolas Cage spend money into existence—all we need is to authorize them to edit some Excel files stored in banks' computers.

Once again, the important question is not whether restrictions can be technically removed but whether they should be removed and the consequences of doing so.

Second, self-imposed restrictions are only an act of self-flagellation if they impede responsible governments from making valuable progress.

If, however, loosening restrictions makes the government behave like Nicolas Cage, then restrictions are not an act of self-flagellation. They're a safety mechanism.

FINAL THOUGHTS

The MMT model is fascinating—it helps us analyze economies from a different lens and even provide an answer to the question, "If you can just print money, why do I pay taxes?" In case you're interested, Appendix A discusses MMT's views on cryptocurrencies such as Bitcoin. Spoiler alert: MMTers don't believe cryptocurrencies have a stable source of value because they can't be used to pay taxes. And they may have a point.

We've identified at least two major weaknesses of MMT. First, many of its most publicized conclusions are obvious. For example, it is not interesting to say that, if a government is allowed to create money, then it cannot run out of money. Second, MMT often omits crucial things, such as how inflation diminishes its claims.

In this chapter, we discussed the hypothetical world proposed by MMT. But MMT makes a big promise. It tells us that MMT describes how many real-world countries operate, despite appearances. For example, the US federal government *already* creates new money on a daily basis to pay for stuff.

If this is true, the consequences are enormous, as we could extrapolate MMT's conclusions to the real world. We could say, for example, that the real-life US government doesn't need taxes to fund its spending and that it cannot run out of money.

Let's see.

CHAPTER TWO

THE REAL WORLD

It is now time to travel back to the real world, where there are rules that limit the government's power to create money. I'm sorry to be such a killjoy!

In the real world, restrictions are imposed to make the government run like a household. The central bank is usually set up as an independent organization whose daily operations cannot be controlled by the ruling government. For example, the Treasury, which is the department in charge of government finances, cannot force the central bank to create new money to cover its spending. This tends to turn the government into just another client of the central bank and a user rather than issuer of the national currency. From now on, for simplicity, whenever I speak of "the government," I will assume the central bank is not part of it but a separate public-purpose organization.

In addition, the central bank is granted political independence. This means it is given certain goals, such as controlling inflation, and it can choose the best tools to do so. Measures are taken to preserve political independence. For example, the US central bank—"the Fed"—is managed by a board of governors from different locations and backgrounds, who meet regularly and vote to make decisions. Governors stay in office for 14 years, which is intended to insulate them from pressure by the current administration.

At first sight, these restrictions seem to make MMT not applicable to the real world. So, why even bother with MMT?

Not so fast!

One of the major contributions of MMT is a detailed analysis of the monetary operations between the US federal government and the Fed. Through its analysis, MMT seeks to prove that, despite appearances, the United States already "does MMT." So, the Fed is not independent like we think. In fact, the US government makes the Fed create money on its behalf on a daily basis to cover its spending. Just like in the MMT world, the real-life US government already creates money all the time to pay its bills! You just need to analyze operations more carefully to see the truth.

While MMT's analysis is heavily US-focused, its conclusions are far-reaching. The United States is often cited as a successful example of central bank independence that others should follow. If the United States is indeed an MMT-style country instead, then MMT is not just relevant to the United States but also to all those countries trying to follow its lead.

Sometimes MMT supplements its analysis by describing operations in other countries, such as the United Kingdom and Australia, which are also revealed to be MMT-like. This strengthens the view that MMT is a useful model for the real world.

If what MMT says is true, then its conclusions become much more interesting and surprising. For example, instead of saying, "A government that can create money cannot run out of money," we can say, "The US government cannot run out of money."

In this chapter, we will study MMT's arguments. We will analyze the two main restrictions that limit the government's power to create money, and we'll see why MMT says these restrictions are not really enforced. We will not discuss the topic of quantitative easing for now, which is a controversial policy implemented by real-world central banks. This topic deserves its own chapter, so we leave it for later.

Let's get started!

RESTRICTION 1: THE GOVERNMENT CAN'T SPEND WHAT IT DOESN'T HAVE

The US government does all its spending from ordinary bank accounts, very much like the rest of us. By "ordinary," I mean that the bank account has a balance in it that is reduced when the government spends and increased when it receives payments. When the government spends $100, its account balance is reduced by $100, and the recipient's account balance is increased by $100. No new money is created or destroyed. This is all done digitally by editing databases that look like giant Excel spreadsheets. This is just like an ordinary bank transfer between you and I—money moves around by adding and subtracting numbers in Excel spreadsheets, and no money is created or destroyed.

The government cannot spend money if its bank account is empty. So, it must replenish it before it can spend. It does so either by collecting taxes or by borrowing money from the public. As a result, we could say that taxes and borrowing fund government spending. The government must carefully plan its budgets to make sure its accounts are replenished before it can spend. This is very unlike the MMT world, where taxes and borrowing aren't required prior to spending, and it's very much like ordinary households.

Let's discuss how this works in a bit more detail. The central government has multiple bank accounts at commercial banks, such as HSBC.[1] These accounts are similar to ordinary accounts that you and I can have at HSBC.

In addition, the US federal government has an account at the central bank, known as the Treasury General Account, or TGA. Only selected institutions are allowed to have bank accounts at the central bank, and the government is one of them. (This might change—central banks around the world are discussing letting ordinary people have accounts with them, which is known as central bank digital currency.)

The TGA also works like an ordinary bank account. If the government sends $100 from the TGA to Smith Engineering, it must have at least $100 in the TGA. After the transfer, the TGA balance drops by $100 and Smith Engineer's balance, say, at HSBC, goes up by $100.

MMT denies that this is how things work. It says that, contrary to appearances, the real-life US government creates new money when it spends, just like in the MMT world. So, it doesn't need to have a positive balance in its account in order to spend, and it doesn't need to replenish its accounts by collecting taxes or selling bonds. The government can spend regardless of any tax collection or borrowing. In other words, all I've just told you is false.

Let's review MMT's arguments.

Invisible Money

Imagine I tell you I have the power to create money. You don't believe me? Just look at your PayPal account. You'll see I've just sent you $100. A new $100 has *appeared* in your account, which proves that I can create money, right?

You wouldn't take me seriously if I told you this. You would argue that, in order to make $100 appear in your account, I must have made $100 disappear from mine. In addition, I can't send the money unless I have at least $100 in my account. This is a money transfer, not money creation—money just moves around, and the total amount of money in existence remains unchanged. My mistake is only counting half of the transaction—the credit into your account—while ignoring the other half—the debit from my account. This gives the illusion of money creation.

Let's go back to MMT. Suppose the government spends $100. Afterward, the private sector finds itself with an extra $100. MMT concludes that the government creates new money when it spends because a new $100 "appears" in private accounts. As a result, the government doesn't need to top up its accounts prior to spending, as it just spends money into existence. The real world is just like MMT!

This argument is echoed all over the MMT literature, and we'll see examples in a second. But let's first clarify why it's wrong.

MMT falls prey to the "invisible money" problem, as in the previous PayPal transfer story. It ignores that the government debits $100 from its account when it credits $100 to someone else. Half of the transaction goes missing from the analysis. Because the debit isn't counted, it seems as if the government created money.

MMT critic Brett Fiebiger explains:

> The laws of mathematics no longer apply (i.e., one credit to private accounts plus one debit to the Treasury's accounts equals money creation) ... It would make a massive difference if the Treasury could directly credit private bank accounts *without having its own account debited:* that would be money creation ... Proponents [of MMT] are not prophets of "truth" but of alternative-world maths.[2]

Let's see a few examples of how the invisible money problem permeates the MMT literature. MMT proponent William Mitchell explains:

> When the recipients of the cheques (sellers of goods and services to the government) deposit the cheques in their bank ... credit entries appear in accounts throughout the commercial banking system. In other words, government spends simply by crediting a private sector bank account.[3]

Mitchell ignores that when new credit "appears" in the private sector, the same amount disappears from the government sector. By the same logic, Mitchell can create money because he can make a new $100 "appear" in your PayPal account by sending you $100 from his account. Mitchell continues:

> Operationally, this process is independent of any prior revenue, including taxing and borrowing. Nor does the account crediting in any way reduce or otherwise diminish any government asset or government's ability to further spend.[4]

This is incorrect. Crediting the payee reduces the government's own bank balance. If Mitchell sends you money via PayPal, his PayPal balance goes down and so does his ability to spend.

Mitchell applies the same logic to tax collection:

> When taxation is paid by private sector cheques (or bank transfers) that are drawn on private accounts in the member banks, the central bank debits a private sector bank account. No real resources are transferred to government. Nor is government's ability to spend augmented by the debiting of private bank accounts.[5]

This is incorrect. It ignores that, when a private account is debited to pay tax, the government's account is credited with an equal amount.

MMTer Stephanie Kelton also echoes the problem in her book *The Deficit Myth*. She says:

> Once Congress authorizes the spending, agencies like the Department of Defense are given permission to enter into contracts with companies like Boeing, Lockheed Martin, and so on. To provision itself with F-35 fighters, the US Treasury instructs its bank, the Federal Reserve, to carry out the payment on its behalf. The Fed does this by marking up the numbers in Lockheed's bank account. Congress doesn't need to "find the money" to spend it. It needs to find the votes! Once it has the votes, it can authorize the spending. The rest is just accounting. As the checks go out, the Federal Reserve clears the payments by crediting the sellers' account with the appropriate number of digital dollars.[6]

Kelton forgets to mention that the government's account is debited when the government pays for the fighter jets. Half of the transaction goes missing in Kelton's analysis. Note that she still published this analysis even though she'd been made aware of its flaw long before.[7]

MMTer Randall Wray takes this problem to a whole new level. He says that the US government doesn't need to worry about hitting its debt ceiling, which is a limit on its total debt imposed by Congress. Wray argues that, after reaching the ceiling, the government "would continue to spend by crediting bank accounts of recipients."[8] Wray ignores the fact that the government must debit its account and have sufficient funds in it before it can continue spending. This is some dangerous advice.

Why is MMT so wrong about something so simple?

It seems MMTers have been thrown off by how statisticians calculate and report the total amount of money in existence in the economy, known as a *monetary aggregate*. One of the most popular monetary aggregates, called M1, shows how much money is held by the private sector. So, when statisticians calculate M1, they ignore bank accounts that belong to the government. For example, M1 does not count the central government's balance at HSBC, but it does count the balance of a private individual at HSBC. For the statisticians who calculate M1, the government's money is invisible.

So, when the government spends, the value of M1 goes up, as the money that was out of sight becomes visible to statisticians—it goes from a government account (not counted in M1) to a private account (counted in M1). Conversely, when the government collects taxes, M1 goes down because the money that was visible becomes hidden.

By only looking at M1, MMTers get the impression that money is created and destroyed when the government spends and collects taxes. In reality, the total amount of money—counting both the money inside private bank accounts and government bank accounts—remains unchanged.

Stephanie Kelton explains:

Bank money (M1) is destroyed when demand deposits are used to pay taxes ... Viewed this way, it can be convincingly argued that the *money* collected from taxation and bond sales cannot possibly finance the government's spending. This is because in order to "get its hands on" the proceeds from taxation and bond sales, the government must destroy the money it has collected. Clearly, government spending cannot be financed by money that is destroyed when received in payment to the State![9]

Kelton thinks that money disappears when the value of M1 goes down. In reality, the money that "disappears" from M1 is recorded as an equal increase in a bank account owned by the central government.

MMT critic Brett Fiebiger explains:

In MMT "money" is only "money" if statisticians "count" it. That the Treasury's cash holdings and deposits at the Fed are not counted in *any* money stock does not mean these items are akin to "non-money." These items exist as "money" where it matters the most: on the books of the Treasury ... and the central bank.[10]

Fiebiger wrote a heated article explaining MMT's mistake and invited MMTers to respond. Seven weeks later, a group of MMTers—Scott Fullwiler, Stephanie Kelton, and Randall Wray—wrote a response. Unfortunately, the response article does not address the points raised by Fiebiger. In the beginning, it says, "Instead of providing a point-by-point response ... , we think it will be more useful to briefly lay-out our main argument in a way that should be accessible ..."[11]

The article starts by explaining the hypothetical MMT world all over again, as discussed in the previous chapter. Afterward, it briefly acknowledges that the real-life United States is different because the government must replenish its accounts before it can spend. However, according to the article, this doesn't make any difference. Why not? Because the money that the government receives today to replenish its account at the Fed must have been created—at some point in the past—by the Fed, which is a branch of "the government."[12] It's hard to see how this argument supports MMT's conclusion in any way.

Brett Fiebiger considers this argument unsatisfactory and complains that MMTers didn't make a "solitary reference" to his original points "in their five-thousand word response." He adds:

> It is difficult to see how progress on academic debates can occur without explicit and specific references to the disputed subject matters (including quotations where appropriate). This is especially the case when the purpose of writing a *response* paper is to *respond* to the work of critics.[13]

Things aren't looking great for MMT. Its argument fell apart very quickly, and MMTers haven't done a great job at defending it. However, I ask you not to dismiss the entire theory right away, for two reasons.

First, there are other arguments to claim that, in practice, the real would may be closer than we think to the MMT world. We'll cover them next. Some of them are deeply flawed, but they help us learn interesting things about modern institutions—and they're hilarious. Other arguments should be taken more seriously, especially those surrounding quantitative easing, which some people believe may have made the MMT world eerily real.

Second, MMT has a lot to say about other important things, such as unemployment and inflation, and it proposes ways of tackling prominent societal challenges. The merits of these proposals are worth analyzing separately, which we'll do later in this book.

The Trillion-dollar Coin

In 2011, a commenter in an MMT blog had a crazy idea. What if the US government created a trillion-dollar platinum coin—out of the blue—and used it to pay its debts? The idea became viral and made it to the news.[14]

In the United States, coins are created by a bureau called the US Mint. The Mint is not allowed to create any coins it wishes. Instead, the Fed tells the Mint which coins to create. So, for all practical purposes, the Fed controls the supply of coins.

There is a loophole though. A 1996 law allowed the Mint to create platinum coins at its own discretion. These coins are intended to be used as *bullion coins*, which means they're valued by investors and collectors due to the weight and fineness of their metal. But the law did not specify which monetary value should be stamped on these coins. So, technically, it is possible for the Mint to produce a platinum coin that contains $1,000 worth of platinum but says "one trillion dollars" on it—all of this without the Fed's approval.

MMTers quickly jumped to the conclusion that the US government could use this loophole to spend without restrictions. They took the conclusion even further—the Fed would have to accept the trillion-dollar coin as a deposit to replenish the TGA with newly created digital money. MMTer Éric Tymoigne explains:

> The Treasury can issue coins (or notes) of any denomination (like a trillion-dollar platinum coin) and transfer them to the Federal Reserve against credit at its TGA.[15]

It soon became clear, however, that the government would find it difficult to have this coin accepted at face value by the public for payments, let alone by the Fed. Moreover, it didn't seem like the government could legally compel its acceptance. Former Mint director Edmund Moy explained:

> It may be legal to mint a platinum bullion coin with a $1 trillion face value, but it's not legal to pass it off as actually worth $1 trillion if there isn't $1 trillion of platinum in it. That's because it's a bullion coin and not a legal circulating coin.[16]

Four days later, the Treasury issued a statement saying:

> Neither the Treasury Department nor the Federal Reserve believes that the law can or should be used to facilitate the production of platinum coins for the purpose of avoiding an increase in the debt limit.[17]

This settled the debate at the time.

Let me add two comments to this. First, it seems MMTers have finally accepted that the government *does* have to replenish its accounts before it can spend—and they're now suggesting creative ways of doing so.

Second, MMTers promised time and again that their theory was *general*—it was the best way to analyze the real-life US economy and those of many other countries around the world. However, the theory seems to rely on progressively narrower exceptions. The story of the trillion-dollar platinum coin is based on a US-centric loophole. This doesn't make MMT sound as general a theory as promised.

We've established that, contrary to what MMT says, the US government *does* need to replenish its accounts—it cannot spend money it doesn't have. But this isn't the end of the discussion. What if, in practice, the central bank gave unlimited loans to the government, helping it replenish its accounts generously? Let's take a deeper look at the relationship between the government and the central bank.

RESTRICTION 2: THE GOVERNMENT CAN'T BORROW FROM THE CENTRAL BANK

Suppose a guy called John works for HSBC. His job is to evaluate the risk of giving loans to customers based on their income, credit score, previous debt, and so on. It turns out that John is Nicolas Cage's close cousin. One day, Nicolas Cage turns up at HSBC and asks for a loan to buy a tenth Rolls Royce. Will HSBC put John in charge of the decision? Probably not. Due to their closeness, HSBC may fear John won't be objective and approve his cousin's loan too easily.

The government must replenish its accounts before it can spend. But what if it could do so by borrowing money from a close cousin—the central bank?

If the central bank were objective, it would carefully analyze whether it's a good idea to give a loan to the government, and it may decide not to do so at all. But people are afraid the central bank will not be objective, just like in the case of Nicolas Cage's cousin. The central bank could even facilitate loans unconditionally to help the government spend as much as it wants.

The central bank creates new money when it lends—it just replaces the borrower's bank balance with a higher number inside a computer.[18] If the central bank does this unconditionally, it makes the real world identical to the MMT world for all practical purposes. This is because the government can effectively spend money into existence in two steps—it first orders the central bank to top up its account with a "loan" of newly created money, and then it spends the money. When the "loan" comes due, it orders the central bank to top up its account again so it can repay the loan, and so on. The central bank is thus controlled by the government, just like in the MMT world.

This arrangement isn't unheard of. For example, in the 2010s and early 2020s, the Argentine central bank kept lending increasingly more money to the government by topping up its bank balance at the click of a button, without too many restrictions. The loans were high enough for the government to repay its previous "loans" and spend more.

To preserve objectivity, central banks usually do *not* give loans to the government. In practice, this means that, when the government runs an auction to sell bonds, the central bank will never buy any. In some cases, the law forbids the central bank to do so. For example, in the United States, it's been illegal since 1935 for the Fed to buy bonds auctioned by the government.[19] In other cases, the law is unwritten—the central bank is technically allowed to buy government bonds at auction but will simply not do so to preserve its independence and reputation. This is the case in the United Kingdom, which has never bought government bonds at auction in recent history, despite no law explicitly preventing it.

If the government wants to borrow money, it must do so by selling bonds to the private sector instead, which is expected to be more objective and freer from political pressure. Just like you and I must prove our creditworthiness to borrow money, the government must convince the private sector that its bonds are worth buying, and there is no risk in doing so. Otherwise, it will struggle to borrow money or might have to a pay a very high interest for it.

Note that the central bank may sometimes choose to buy government bonds—and other stuff—on resale from the private sector. The central bank may do this to try to influence the behavior of the private sector and control inflation. We'll get back to this point in the next chapter. Either way, the government must still sell bonds to the private sector first.

MMT says that this is all a smoke screen. If you carefully look into all the operations, you realize that the US government can routinely borrow as much as it wants from the central bank. So, the United States lives in the MMT world, as the government can access as much newly created money as it wants behind the scenes.

Let's quickly explore MMT's arguments.

But Government Checks Don't Bounce!

Let me tell you something personal: My checks never bounce. If I hand you a check, you'll see you can deposit it into your bank without any issues. That must mean I'm in cahoots with my bank, right? Not really! The reason my checks don't bounce is that I never write a check if I don't have the necessary funds in my account.

As it turns out, checks written by the central government don't usually bounce either. MMTers argue that this somehow proves that the central bank provides unconditional funding to the government. MMT proponent Randall Wray explains:

> In the US, complex procedures have been adopted to ensure that treasury can spend by cutting checks; that treasury checks never "bounce."[20]

He adds:

> The Treasury coordinates operations with the central bank to ensure its checks don't bounce ... The evidence that the central bank and Treasury do coordinate in this way is that central banks hit their rate targets and that Treasury checks don't bounce.[21]

MMT hasn't yet explained what such procedure is. In reality, the Fed isn't mandated to prevent government checks from bouncing.[22] In fact, the government is not allowed to have an overdraft—or a negative balance—in the TGA.[23] So, if it tries to spend more money than it has in there, its checks will bounce unless current rules change.

Moreover, the fact that checks don't bounce isn't a reason to be suspicious of some sort of collusion. It's just proof that the government only writes checks when it has the funds to pay for them. After all, my checks don't bounce either, and it's not because I'm in cahoots with my bank.

Emergencies

MMTers think the government and the central bank will collude to get around restrictions should the need arise, and they cite historical examples of this. Éric Tymoigne explains:

At the request of the Federal Reserve, which needed help to preserve stability in the money market, the 1942 Second War Powers Act removed the 1935 restriction subject to reapproval by Congress every two years ... The Act allowed the outstanding amount of treasuries directly purchased by the Federal Reserve to be at most $5 billion at any time ... The Board kept that power until the end of 1983.[24]

More recently, MMT sympathizer Steve Keen notes that, during the COVID-19 pandemic, the Bank of England authorized the UK government to borrow money directly from it by using a special account for that purpose.[25]

There are a few issues with MMT's argument. First, emergency loans are limited. In the case of WW2 cited by Éric Tymoigne, the Fed was limited to buying a maximum of five billion dollars worth of bonds directly from the government. In the COVID-19 case, the Bank of England only authorized temporary loans provided that the government would pay them back promptly.[26]

In addition, wars and pandemics are exceptional situations. What if the government decided to increase its spending in a business-as-usual context? Would the Fed provide direct access to loans to facilitate it? Officially, the answer is no, and there are no rules that compel the Fed to give unconditional loans to the government—quite the opposite.

For the MMT model to apply, the government should be able to self-declare an emergency unilaterally, and the central bank would have to lend it money—no questions asked. Only in that case would the government be able to plan its budgets as if money wasn't a problem.

All in all, MMT has failed to prove that the second restriction—that the government cannot borrow directly from the central bank—is an illusion. As it stands today, the government cannot knock on the central bank's door and obtain an unconditional loan—no questions asked.

WHAT'S THE POINT?

MMTers have gone to great lengths to try to prove that the real-world United States operates just like the MMT world. But if that's indeed the case, why do they bother so much to prove it? After all, if both views of the world are equivalent, why does it matter to adopt one or the other?

To understand the reason, we need to distinguish two components of MMT. One is a description of how operations are physically carried out, such as the fact that the government spends by creating money on a daily basis. The other component is a set of policy recommendations. For example, MMT recommends that the government should not worry about "running out of money," and it should provide a guaranteed job for everyone who wants one.

MMT tries to prove that the real-life US government already "does MMT" in the first, "physical" sense.[27] My impression is that the point of this analysis is to tell us, "We're halfway there." So, we could easily do MMT "all the way," including implementing its recommended policies, as much of the work is already done. For example, the US government could implement a job guarantee program tomorrow without worrying about "finding the money," as it *already* creates money on a daily basis to cover its spending.

But why are politicians so deluded? Why do they keep budgeting like households if they don't have to? Why pretend you can run out of money when you're constantly creating it to pay for whatever you want? According to MMTers, many politicians are philosophically opposed to helping people, and they rely on the excuse of "not having enough money" to justify it. So, the "household" view is just a big ruse used by politicians to justify their lack of generosity. Stephanie Kelton explains:

> Why not stop pretending that Congress needs to budget like a household? The truth is, many lawmakers find the self-imposed constraints politically useful.

For one thing, members of Congress routinely face pressure from voters seeking more generous funding for health care, education, and so on. The budget rules give them political cover. Instead of explaining that they're philosophically opposed to boosting Pell Grant funding to help low-income students attend college, lawmakers can feign empathy with their constituents while claiming their hands are tied because of the deficit. If they couldn't hide behind *the deficit myth*, what excuse would they use to justify withholding support? It helps to have a bad cop.[28]

MMTer Éric Tymoigne explains, "Many policymakers and citizens, for a range of reasons and beliefs, want less government involvement in the economy." He adds that the "we-don't-have-money card" is proven irrelevant by MMT.[29]

Similarly, William Mitchell suggests that the current, "household" view is the result of ideology, and the MMT helps remove it. He says, "In Marxist terms, we are stripping back the 'veil of ideology.'"[30]

Note, however, that MMT's most prominent critics do *not* want smaller government. In fact, they want many of the same things MMTers want, including bigger government. However, they think MMT is the wrong framework to attain those goals. One of them is Brett Fiebiger, a fierce MMT critic whom we cited earlier. He says, "There is no debate that all of the policy constraints imposed on the Treasury's activities are arbitrary and should be abolished."[31] So, he wants to remove spending restrictions, just like MMTers. However, he thinks "MMT is a distraction to understanding and developing solutions to current economic problems."[32]

Another fierce MMT critic, economist Thomas Palley, advocates government generosity, just like MMTers, but doesn't think MMT is accurate. He says, "In the current moment of high unemployment, MMT makes a valuable contribution as part of the rhetoric advocating expansionary fiscal policy. However, as regards macroeconomic theory, MMT adds nothing new warranting its own label. Instead, its over-simplifications represent a step-back in understanding."[33]

Policy analyst Matt Bruenig, who is an advocate for democratic socialism and the welfare state, adds, "The real point of MMT seems to be to deploy misleading rhetoric with the goal of deceiving the public about the necessity of taxes."[34]

FINAL THOUGHTS

MMT proponent Randall Wray writes:

> The problem is that the critics [of MMT] almost universally have no idea how the government actually spends; they have no understanding of the operational details and coordination between the Fed and the Treasury that allows government to spend, collect taxes, and sell bonds.[35]

After such a statement, we would perhaps expect MMT to provide a thorough and correct description of operational details. Instead, MMT's description is riddled with mistakes. Some of them are pretty grave, such as forgetting to count some money and claiming it doesn't exist. MMT critic Thomas Palley says, "MMT is a mix of old and new, the old is correct and well understood, while the new is substantially wrong."[36] This chapter gives us a hint of why Palley feels this way.

Even if we decided to unshackle government spending, just like MMTers want, I'm not sure I would put them in charge of running the show. They don't seem to analyze the real world accurately, and they tend to respond to criticism only with more erroneous points.

In case you're interested, Appendix B debunks more of MMT's arguments about "the real world." For example, MMT provides a sophisticated explanation of why the US government still sells bonds even though it doesn't need to ever borrow money. The appendix shows that the entire argument relies, once again, on failing to count transactions properly. If you're a bit nerdy, you may want to check out a part of the appendix in which I go through banking balance sheets to debunk another one of MMT's arguments. To the best of my knowledge, this chapter and its appendix cover all MMT's arguments about why the MMT world is identical to the real world—and they all suffer from severe glitches.

And now let's turn to the elephant in the room.

After the 2008 crisis, central banks around the world started buying astronomical quantities of government bonds on resale from the private sector, and they created money to pay for them. Many people have become suspicious that, in practice, central banks have been indirectly funding government spending, a bit like Nicolas Cage getting unlimited loans from HSBC—approved by his cousin who works there. This rings MMT bells. Has the government finally found a sneaky way to get around its spending limits? Let's see.

CHAPTER THREE

QUANTITATIVE EASING

In the early 2000s, economists thought they had it all under control. Over the previous two decades, high-income countries such as the United States, the United Kingdom, Canada, and France had experienced remarkably high economic stability.[1] This was attributed to central bank independence and effective inflation control. In 2002, two economists named this era "the Great Moderation,"[2] and the term soon became widely popular.

But this naming may have been a bit premature. In 2008, economies collapsed all around the world. The ensuing period, known as the Great Recession, was the most severe global economic slump since the 1930s.

Due to the notoriously reduced economic activity, central banks started fearing *deflation*, which means a generalized decrease in prices. This may sound good at first—who doesn't want to pay less for stuff?—but economists were terrified of it. They feared that, if prices started going down, people would postpone consumption to enjoy lower prices—why not wait a little longer to buy that fridge or book that holiday? Economists feared that the resulting lack of consumption could depress economic activity even further and make the existing recession even worse.

So, in the wake of the 2008 crisis, central banks wanted prices to go up—they wanted to generate inflation. For that, they had to encourage people to spend more. They tried conventional mechanisms for this, but they didn't work well enough.[3] It was time to take unconventional measures.

Central banks around the world resorted to a tool called *quantitative easing*, or QE, which is intended to increase inflation when other tools aren't working. While QE had been used to some extent in Japan before, it was completely novel for most central banks. While intended to be a temporary measure, the tool was also used for many years and ramped up at a dramatic scale during the COVID-19 pandemic.

QE involves a lot of money creation, so many people have compared it to MMT. Could QE be a disguised form of MMT? Could it be that MMT has been slowly creeping into our lives—in the form of QE—without us realizing it?

In this chapter, we'll explore QE and its relationship to MMT. We'll first go through the official QE story, and we'll then discuss why some people have become a bit cynical and think there's more to it.

This chapter concludes our analysis of the MMT world versus the real world. Afterward, we will move on to the topic of policy—can the government use its power to create money to do good, without causing a mess?

HOW TO GENERATE INFLATION

Imagine you wanted to generate inflation. You could create new money and put it in the pocket of consumers all around the economy, perhaps by handing out $1,000 to each resident. This could make people spend more and thus push prices up. Economists aren't big fans of this idea, as they think it could cause all sorts of problems. For example, consumers could spend the money too quickly, making inflation go out of control. In addition, it would be hard to revert, as you can't just tell people to give you the $1,000 back.

Instead, QE tries to generate inflation in a subtler way. Instead of targeting consumers, it targets risk-averse investors by encouraging them to take more risks. The central bank hopes that increased risk-taking will cause more spending across the economy and generate inflation.

QE has a lot to do with government bonds. If you remember, these are certificates issued by the government that say "I owe you" and entitle the holder to receive a payment from the government on a certain future date. The government issues bonds when it wants to borrow money from the private sector to top up its accounts.

Financial institutions, such as pension funds, usually own a lot of government bonds, as these are considered very safe investments. Clinging to government bonds is a way to play it safe—the investment manager just buys government bonds and passively waits to collect interests. QE is designed to discourage this behavior.

It works as follows. The central bank announces it will spend a large amount of money on buying government bonds on resale from private markets. This pushes up the price of these bonds. Their owners, such as pension funds, are thus motivated to sell them to the central bank.

After collecting the proceeds from the sales, financial institutions find themselves with money in their accounts. What will they do with it? The central bank hopes financial institutions will invest it in riskier ways instead of clinging to dull government bonds. The Bank of England explains:

> Purchases have been targeted towards long-term assets held by non-bank financial institutions, like insurers and pension funds, who may be encouraged to use the funds to invest in other, riskier assets like corporate bonds and equities.[4]

The central bank hopes this will cause inflation in at least two ways. First, financial institutions may become likelier to invest in business endeavors, for example, by buying risky corporate bonds. This will make it easier for businesses to borrow money and thus conduct more projects and spend more. According to the Bank of England, even businesses with a low-quality credit record may find it easier to borrow money thanks to QE.[5]

During the height of QE, there was a surge of investment in venture capital funds, which are funds that invest in risky technology start-ups. At that time, many investors told me that safe assets like government bonds had become expensive—as the central bank was buying them in huge quantities—so they had no choice but to make riskier bets. That's why they turned to venture capital.

Second, the central bank hopes QE will make households spend more money.[6] Suppose pension funds, after they sell their government bonds to the central bank, use the proceeds to buy Apple stock. This makes the price of Apple stock go up. If you've invested in Apple yourself, you'll feel wealthier. This could make you spend more and thus stoke inflation. For example, after seeing the price of Apple stock go up, you'll feel rich and go on that holiday you've been dreaming of for a while.

But how can the central bank afford to buy so many government bonds from pension funds, insurance companies, and so on? It's very simple—it just creates the money to pay for it. The central bank just edits numbers in computers to increase the account balances of the bond sellers.

QE was implemented at an astronomical scale. Economist Joseph Gagnon explains:

> Between December 2008 and March 2010, the Federal Reserve purchased more than $1.7 trillion in assets ... We believe that no investor—public or private—has ever accumulated such a large amount of securities in such a short period of time.

While initially intended to be a temporary measure, QE continued at various scales around the world for many years. When the COVID-19 epidemic hit, central banks all over the world became terrified of severe deflation as people stopped spending. So, QE was resumed or ramped up all over the world. And this time it was on steroids—central banks purchased government bonds and other assets at a much higher rate than ever before.

In 2021, inflation soared around the world. Some people thought this was due to COVID-related supply chain disruption and, later, the war in Ukraine. Others thought central banks had overdone QE during the pandemic, which generated too much inflation.[7] Either way, central banks decided to start reverting QE. This meant they slowly started selling back to the private sector the numerous government bonds and other assets they'd bought during QE.[8] Central banks then destroyed the money collected from these sales—they just struck it off the record by lowering numbers in computers. This is known as *quantitative tightening*, or QT. The process is still underway as of this writing, and it's far from finished.

What I've just told you is the *official* story. This is the explanation of QE you'll hear from central banks themselves. But many people aren't convinced that this is the full story. Let's see.

A STRANGE OMISSION

According to the official story, QE makes businesses and households spend more money. But what about the government? Wouldn't the government be affected too?

The government is absent from the official story. A transcribed speech on the Fed's website says that QE affects "the decisions of households and businesses," without mentioning the government.[9] The Bank of England's website does the same.[10]

But some people think that QE has perhaps affected the government too—it has made the government borrow more and spend more.

Suppose the government wants to borrow money. Usually, this requires convincing the private sector to buy its bonds. In the QE era, however, everybody knows that the central bank will buy a large quantity of those bonds on resale. It's as if the central bank was "guaranteeing" demand for these bonds.

This could make the private sector less careful about buying bonds from the government, as it knows it can just resell them to the central bank. This could perhaps encourage the government to borrow and spend more than usual.

Central banks don't seem to see it this way. They assume the government makes decisions independently of the existence of QE. In this view, governments decide how much to spend, how much to tax, and how much to borrow independently of what the central bank is doing with its QE program. This is probably because central banks assume the government plans its budgets wisely. For example, the government knows that QE will one day be reversed, which will make selling bonds more difficult, so it decides not to borrow excessively in the present.

But some people are not convinced. Economic advisor Stephen D. King says:

> Quantitative easing has also reduced the discipline imposed on fiscal policymakers. Although central banks would doubtless claim it as mere coincidence, it's striking that an extended period of quantitative easing was associated with the biggest ever peacetime increase in government debt. Would government debt have risen quite as far without being "underwritten" by central banks? Would finance ministries have been quite so generous in their fiscal largesse, had they had to contend with the risk of significantly higher debt interest payments in the absence of quantitative easing?[11]

Some people have an even more extreme point of view. They think QE does not work in the official way at all—by encouraging businesses and households to spend more. Instead, it works by helping *the government* spend more. British businessman Lord Turner of Ecchinswell explains:

> What QE is doing now is what it has been doing for many years in Japan. It is lubricating a fiscal expansion and making it easy for the Government to run large fiscal deficits.[12]

Investment blogger Lyn Alden thinks the same. She says:

> Things like Medicare, Social Security, military spending, crisis stimulus checks, and so forth, would likely have to be reduced if the Treasury was limited to only borrowing from real lenders rather than borrowing from newly-created pools of dollars from the Federal Reserve.[13]

This idea is no longer just found in informal blogs. It is also spreading around academic circles. Economists have been studying how central bank policies and government actions could be more intertwined than it may seem at first.[14]

Central bankers have also started acknowledging that QE may affect government spending. In 2021, the governor of the Bank of England recognized that "every borrower" benefits from QE, "and every borrower includes the government."[15]

This leaves us with two very different interpretations of QE. One of them—the official story—is that QE just affects the private sector—businesses and households—by encouraging more risk-taking and spending. The other version is that, when the central bank implements QE, it helps *the government* spend more.

When you consider that this is all paid for with newly created money, the latter version sounds a lot like MMT! Could it be that, thanks to QE, the government is able to spend as much as it wants—all of this with newly created money—just like in the MMT world? Let's see.

DOES QE = MMT?

In the MMT world, the government faces no spending limits. It can keep spending increasingly more, and ideally, it will only stop spending voluntarily when it thinks it could cause inflation.

As discussed in the previous chapter, the real world is different. The government is limited in its spending by financial factors, such as the amount of money in its account and its capacity to borrow more.

But does QE change this? Does it remove the government's spending limits, bringing it closer to the MMT world?

Once again, there are two answers to this question—an official one and an unofficial one.

The official answer is "no," QE does not remove spending limits. This is because QE is only used in limited quantities at the discretion of the central bank. So, the government cannot count on it. For example, the central bank may decide to "only" buy $100 billion worth of government bonds just when the government wants to spend an additional $500 billion. So, the government would have to raise taxes or convince the private sector to lend it the remaining $400 billion—neither of which is easy.

In addition, QE is intended to be a temporary tool used as a last resort to fight deflation. QE is expected to be reverted once the threat of deflation recedes. So, even if QE does indeed help the government spend more, this is only temporary.

So, all in all, QE is an "easing" tool, as its name suggests, but it is not a permanent arrangement that lets the government spend as much money as it wants, whenever it wants.

However, not everyone is convinced by the official story. Some people think QE has sometimes been used and will be increasingly used in unofficial ways to help the government spend increasingly more, thus reducing or eliminating the government's spending limits. For example, the central bank may collude with the government and use QE not to fight deflation but to buy as many bonds as the government wants to sell. The fact that the bonds are bought on resale and not directly from the government becomes just a smokescreen, as everyone in the private sector knows they can buy any number of bonds from the government and resell them immediately to the central bank. If this were to happen, government spending limits would fade away, and we would enter an MMT era.

Economist George Selgin explains:

> The question that concerns us here isn't whether the Fed is presently bound to fund the federal government's expenses, as some Modern Monetary Theorists suggest. The question is whether the Fed, perhaps owing in part to MMT's influence, might be compelled to do so in the future, through explicit legislation or otherwise, and particularly whether its quantitative easing capacity might, or should, be exploited for this purpose.[16]

Some recent, controversial events have made people think we're already on that slippery slope. Let's have a look.

WHATEVER IT TAKES

In the early 2010s, a handful of European countries—Ireland, Greece, Spain, Portugal, and Cyprus—found themselves in trouble. Their governments were deeply indebted, and it didn't seem they'd be able to pay their debts anytime soon. Credit agencies downgraded their credit rating.[17] As a result, fearful investors started asking for higher interest on these countries' government bonds, and some people started to fear that the euro, which is their common currency, would collapse. This situation became known as the European debt crisis.

But then Mario Draghi, the president of the European Central Bank, or ECB, uttered the magic words "whatever it takes." During a speech, he said:

> Within our mandate, the ECB is ready to do whatever it takes to preserve the euro. And believe me, it will be enough.[18]

These magic words were widely interpreted as a commitment by the ECB to use QE to buy government bonds of troubled countries in the resale market.[19] This would make private holders of government bonds feel safer, as they could resell their bonds to the central bank should the need arise. Immediately after the famous speech, investors calmed down and lowered the interest they expected from the troubled countries' government bonds.

A few months later, the ECB announced the specifics of its intended QE program, which was called Outright Monetary Transactions, or OMTs. Compared to ordinary QE, which was performed in limited, predetermined quantities, OMTs were unlimited—the ECB would buy as many government bonds as it considered necessary to intervene the bond market in an effective way.

Officially, the reason for this intervention was not to help troubled governments. Instead, it was to correct an exaggerated perception of risk by private investors. According to the ECB, this perception was unwarranted and was making it hard for the ECB to implement its ordinary inflation-fighting policies.[20] ECB executive Benoît Cœuré explained, "The goal of OMTs is a narrow one: to eliminate the unwarranted and self-reinforcing fears."[21]

To make sure OMTs weren't interpreted as a way to bail out troubled governments, the ECB imposed stringent conditions before OMTs could be activated. For example, the troubled country would first have to obtain financial support from its eurozone peers.[22] As of this writing, OMTs have never been used.

So, officially, the ECB does not *really* intend to do "whatever it takes" because the proposed procedure comes with too many conditions.

Some people, however, aren't convinced by this and think there are other, unwritten rules. Economic advisor Stephen D. King explains:

> The then-president of the European Central Bank issued his "magic words," promising to do "whatever it takes" ... The ECB thus found itself with three—potentially competing—roles: preserver of price stability, lender of last resort and now bond market bailer-out-in-chief ... While the ECB's decision is understandable, it's difficult to see its intervention as anything other than another attempt to "nationalise" parts of the bond market.[23]

If the official view is true, then MMT has little to do with eurozone countries. These countries must budget like households and must convince the private sector that lending to the government is a good idea. However, if the cynical view prevails—the ECB is genuinely willing to do *whatever* it takes—then eurozone countries could spend as much as they want knowing the ECB will rescue them and refinance their debts indefinitely by using QE. It is a world of unlimited bailouts. The cynical view puts these governments in the MMT world because they don't face household-style spending limits.

RISK-FREE

Let me now bring attention to another elephant in the room. Many people describe the bonds issued by the United States, the United Kingdom, and other high-income countries as "risk-free," which means the government will never fail to pay them when they're due. So, they're the safest of all investments.

In 2021, during a QE-related hearing, the governor of the Bank of England said:

> The government bond market plays a much bigger role than just financing the Government; it is also an anchor in financial markets because it is a risk-free asset, so an awful lot of collateral and security in financial markets is government bonds.[24]

The idea that government bonds are "risk-free" is pervasive in the financial literature.

But why are government bonds risk-free?

There are two possible answers. One is that the governments of these high-income countries have a history of planning their budgets carefully to make sure they can always pay their debts. In particular, the government will raise taxes if necessary to make sure debt is repaid promptly. So, they've gained confidence from investors. They're considered risk-free thanks to the government's pristine reputation. Similarly, a bank may consider extending a mortgage to an individual virtually "risk-free" if this individual has a pristine credit record.

Another answer is that there is an unwritten rule that says the central bank will do "whatever it takes" should the need arise. Because these countries issue their own currencies, it's always technically possible for the central bank to use QE or other means to rescue the government by creating money. For example, the central bank can buy any problematic government bonds from private investors, with newly created money, should the need arise. Financial services company Hargreaves Lansdown explains:

> UK Government bonds are typically viewed as one of the "safest" forms of bond. That's because the government usually has significant influence over its currency, so can print more money to pay back investors if it needs to.[25]

If the official answer is the correct one—bonds of these high-income countries are risk-free due to the government's pristine reputation—then MMT doesn't seem very relevant. The government must limit its spending and budget like a household to pay its debts promptly and retain its good reputation.

If the other answer is the right one—the central bank will do "whatever it takes"—then these countries live in something much closer to the MMT world, as the government can spend as much as it wants. The central bank will always have its back—it will be ready to create as much money as needed to make sure the government can always pay its bills.

SUSPICIOUS COORDINATION

When the COVID-19 pandemic hit, governments around the world implemented extraordinary measures to stimulate the economy, including paying a large portion of private sector's wages. To finance this, they took massive amounts of debt by issuing new bonds. At the same time, central banks used a massive amount of QE to stimulate the economy.

So, on the one hand, the government borrowed more money by issuing bonds and selling them to the private sector. On the other hand, the central bank created money to buy government bonds from the private sector. Many people thought it was suspicious that these two things happened simultaneously. It was almost as if the central bank was creating money specifically to help fund increased government spending, with the private sector only being an irrelevant, pass-through intermediary.

For a lot of people, this rang MMT bells. Economist Marc Lavoie says:

> The actions of several Western governments during the COVID-19 pandemic, especially in 2020, appeared to come directly from the MMT bluebook ... While government officials or central bankers were denying that they were now following the prescriptions of MMT, it was difficult to explain in which way these policies and their results differed from those advocated by MMT economists.[26]

What made it all even more suspicious was that, in some cases, the amount of money created by the central bank closely matched the government's increased spending. It seemed as if, for every extra penny of government borrowing, the central bank created one new penny and bought government bonds with it. The central bank is supposed to act independently of the government, and it's not supposed to create money specifically to help fund the government, so many people found this disturbing.

An accusatory *Financial Times* article explained that, in 2020, the Bank of England's QE "perfectly tracked central government's borrowing needs." The article also said that a survey revealed that the majority of bond buyers "believe that QE in its current incarnation works by buying enough bonds to mop up the amount the government issues."[27]

The UK Parliament conducted an extensive investigation on the matter. During the investigation, it invited Governor of the Bank of England Andrew Bailey to answer questions. One of the politicians in the room, Lord Haskel, asked him, "In November 2020 you chose to buy an additional £150 billion of government bonds ... Did you feel it was important to communicate why you chose that amount rather than, for instance, £200 billion or £100 billion?"[28] While the question is formulated in a polite way, Lord Haskel seems to be accusing the central bank of collusion with the government, as the former provided the latter *just* the amount of money it needed to borrow.

Here's an excerpt of Bailey's long-winded response to the question:

> Our judgments on whether it is £150 billion or £200 billion are made to the best of our ability essentially by putting those numbers through our assessment processes and deciding which one of them, in a sense, given all the other analyses we do, is best to take, over the course of the horizon, which typically is up to three years, to have inflation at its target ...
>
> In answer to the question why it was £150 billion, it was driven primarily by the inflation analysis and target, but sitting behind it was also an assessment of the headroom we had to undertake purchases, so we could not have gone at that point in time hugely above that number, frankly.[29]

Bailey seems to imply that the central bank indeed "mopped" up the new bonds issued by the government but not because it wanted to help the government. Instead, the central bank wanted to buy as many bonds as possible to fight deflation, so it bought all of them. The central bank was just doing the maximum possible amount of QE it could.

Another politician in the room, Viscount Chandos, asked Bailey, "Can you say how much and what type of coordination took place between the Bank of England and the Treasury during the pandemic, particularly in the early months?" Again, this sounds like an accusation of suspicious collaboration between the central bank and the government.

Bailey responded:

> I start by saying that we do not use the word "coordination" ... It implies active management of policies jointly, and that does not happen. We tend to use the words "consistent" and "complementary" ...
>
> I can tell you that the Chancellor [who is the head of the Treasury] and I were talking daily at the height of this ... If you asked me what we talked about, I would say two things. At that point, we were basically sharing our assessment of what we were hearing about the economy ... The second thing that dominated our conversations was Covid ... We were both trying to work out what we were hearing from epidemiologists.[30]

After the investigation, the Parliament published a report entitled, "Quantitative easing: A dangerous addiction?" The report concludes:

> The level of detail published by the Bank on how quantitative easing affects the economy is not sufficient to enable Parliament and the public to hold it to account. This has bred distrust.[31]

Once again, if we endorse the official view, then the extensive use of QE during COVID-19 had little to do with MMT. This was because it didn't enable the government to spend in an unlimited way. Instead, it was a tool used independently and temporarily by the central bank to respond to a remarkable emergency. The fact that the central bank "wiped out" all the government's new debt was an independent decision of the central bank for deflation-fighting purposes.

More cynical people, however, have interpreted these events as one step forward along the MMT slippery slope. During the pandemic, central banks around the world created as much money as governments needed to fund their increased spending, which made them very close to how the MMT world works—at least temporarily. Will they be tempted to do more of this in the future?

THE INFAMOUS MINI-BUDGET

In September 2022, something pretty remarkable happened in the United Kingdom. The government announced a tax and spending reform, known as the mini-budget. The reform reduced taxes with the goal of fostering economic growth. At the same time, it *increased* government spending by subsidizing energy costs. So, the government would collect less revenue but spend more. Many people thought the numbers didn't quite add up.

The reason I'm bringing up this story is that it was an interesting test of MMT. I'm sure MMTers wouldn't specifically endorse the measures proposed by the mini-budget. However, the UK government tried to increase its spending without worrying about how to pay for it, which rings MMT bells.

Investors freaked out immediately. They were afraid the government didn't have a credible plan to pay back its debts or that inflation would increase as a result of additional government spending. This caused a sharp drop in the price of government bonds, which means the government would find it much costlier to borrow and thus much more difficult to carry out its plan.

In addition, the central bank had recently announced it would start reverting QE—it would stop buying government bonds and start selling them off instead. So, the central bank didn't seem to have the government's back anymore to facilitate its spending, like it did during the pandemic. This aggravated the sharp drop of government bond prices.

Five days after the infamous mini-budget, the central bank decided to run an unexpected new round of QE to buy government bonds on resale and calm the waters. The central bank explained that this was not to help the government; it was only to provide relief to pension funds which had suffered from the drop in the price of government bonds. The Bank explained, "These purchases will be strictly time limited. They are intended to tackle a specific problem in the long-dated government bond market."[32]

For a moment, it seemed as if the central bank was rescuing the government by using QE—it bought the disgraced government bonds just to help the government fund its questionable budget.[33] But the Bank of England kept its promise. It only ran QE for a limited amount of time. Afterward, it went on with its plans to reverse QE, thus stopping bond purchases. In addition, it took actions to increase stability of pension funds and prevent this kind of rescue in the future.[34]

The UK government had to reverse the mini-budget, and the prime minister resigned as a result. Since then, UK governments have been more diligent in planning their budgets, and they've been speaking of "plugging holes" in government finances.[35] The "household" approach is back on. The UK's MMT-style experiment failed.

FINAL THOUGHTS

In theory, it is hard to argue that QE equals MMT. This is because QE is used at the discretion of the central bank—not the government—and it's intended to be a temporary tool only used as a last resort.

However, things may not be that simple, as the actions of the central bank may influence the government and vice versa. In addition, some people fear that QE may be used in an unofficial way to facilitate government spending or rescue deeply indebted governments. The more this happens, the more QE takes us along the MMT route. Let's keep an eye out! We should be particularly wary of expressions such as "whatever it takes" or "risk-free."

In case you're interested, Appendix C discusses how MMTers themselves see QE. Spoiler alert: they think it's an ineffective and undemocratic policy. If anybody should be "printing money," it should be the democratically elected government, which would hopefully follow MMT-recommended policies to do good for the economy.

Enough of the real world! Let's now move on to the important topic of policy, which will be our focus for the remainder of the book. Let's give MMT the benefit of the doubt and assume we let the government create money the MMT way. What sort of good can the government do with this power? And how can we make sure it doesn't make a mess? Let's start with the elephant in the room: inflation. What does MMT say about inflation, and how can the government create money without causing an Argentine-style or even Zimbabwe-style inflation debacle?

CHAPTER FOUR

INFLATION

I remember vividly something that happened when I was in the fourth grade, back in Argentina where I grew up. In our school, there was a small cafeteria where we could buy snacks during breaks. I was a big fan of jelly beans. To buy them, you had to tell the lady at the counter how much you wanted to spend, and she would scoop out the corresponding number of jelly beans from a large box and put them in a plastic bag for you.

One day, I turned up at the cafeteria and told her I wanted one peso worth of jelly beans (I actually said it in Spanish—*"un peso"*). One peso meant a gigantic bag of jelly beans, and it was rare for anyone to order as much. The lady opened her eyes widely and yelled "ONE PESO?!" in front of everyone else at the shop. Heads turned.

One of the reasons I remember this event so vividly is that it was pretty embarrassing—she accused me of gluttony in front of all the other kids.

But there's another reason why this memory keeps popping up. It reminds me that one peso used to have the power to buy a lot of stuff. This is no longer the case. As of this writing, prices in Argentina have multiplied by a factor of 1,600 since my jelly bean incident—in a span of 24 years. You can't even buy a single jelly bean with one peso nowadays. I don't think you can actually buy anything with one peso. In foreign exchange markets, one peso is now worth 0.00085 US dollars.

At first, the increase in prices was slow and moderate. By my last year of high school, prices had "only" multiplied by three since the jelly bean incident. Prices started to go up at a much faster rate when I went to university, and it became pretty noticeable in everyday life. People became frustrated and started speaking about *inflation*, a phenomenon in which prices go up over time or, equivalently, the value of money goes down.

The government tried to fight inflation through *price controls*, which meant it tried to strike deals with supermarkets to guarantee that the prices of certain products wouldn't rise. But you could never find those products on the shelves.

Argentineans couldn't save money using the national currency, as it lost its value pretty quickly. So, they tried to exchange any spare cash for US dollars. This caused all sorts of problems. The government implemented *exchange controls*, which meant it limited foreign exchange transactions by law. You could only buy a limited number of US dollars every month, and even this required a special authorization, or you'd be turned down at the exchange bureau. If you wanted to buy currency to travel abroad, you had to bring in your tickets to prove it. Even then, exchange bureaus struggled to approve your transaction, as the software used for it only worked a few minutes every day.

Exchange controls didn't solve the issue. A gigantic black market for US dollars developed, and it was completely overt. Argentineans euphemistically called it the "blue" market.

This isn't the first time it happened. Argentina has suffered from multiple bouts of high inflation, just like many of its Latin American neighbors. Dramatic episodes of inflation have also taken place all over the world, including the notorious inflation in Germany in the 1920s and in Zimbabwe in the 2000s. If you remember, that also happened in the Massachusetts colony, which we discussed in Chapter 1. Prices kept going up and up in the colony, until paper money, which the government kept creating at ever-increasing rates, was outlawed and replaced by silver coins. Inflation also made a stellar comeback all over the world in 2021, even in places where it was least expected.

One thing these episodes have in common is that, as they unfolded, the government was funding a lot of its spending by creating new money. This has made a lot of people uneasy about MMT—what if MMT is a recipe for inflationary disaster?

In this chapter, we'll first discuss MMT's explanation of inflation—why it happens, how to control it, and its relationship to the creation of money. We'll then see how MMT analyzes previous episodes of inflation in the real world, including the infamous cases of Germany and Zimbabwe, as well as the 2021 global inflation. We'll finish by commenting on why inflation matters.

THE ON/OFF SWITCH

In April 2025, one of my friends booked a ticket to Rome to spend a quiet offseason holiday. She didn't book accommodation in advance, as availability seemed plentiful and prices were favorable. But five days before her trip, the Pope died. When she searched for a hotel room, she was in for a big surprise.

In the days after the Pope's death, the price of accommodation soared around Rome, as numerous people traveled to attend the funeral. The city registered one of the highest average room rates on record. Hotel occupancy went all the way up to 88% on the night before the funeral.[1] As it turns out, when people start spending more on something, its price can go up as a result.

In this case, the increase in prices was localized and temporary. But what if there's a more generalized bout of spending around the economy? What if spending around the wider economy increases in a noticeable way?

A wider surge in spending could come from the private sector. For example, companies may become excited about a new technology and invest in it. It could also come for the public sector—think of a new infrastructure project or a stimulus package.

Economists think that large increases in spending can cause inflation, just like hotel prices went up in Rome but on a wider scale. Inflation can thus be the result of "too much spending" around the economy.

MMT endorses this view. However, it provides an unusual explanation of *when* more spending can cause inflation. According to MMT, it all comes down to *slack*.

An economy has slack when it has unused, idle capacity to produce more stuff. For example, there are unused machines, unemployed workers, and piles of spare materials. MMT says that, if there is any level of slack, producers react to a surge of spending by producing more stuff—they turn on their idle machines, hire more workers, dig into their spare materials, and so on. They do not increase prices. So, in an economy with any spare capacity, more spending is quenched with more products and services, not with price hikes.[2]

Things are different when there is no slack in the economy. Imagine all machines are already used at full capacity, there is no unemployment, and there are no materials lying around. In this case, according to MMT, producers respond to a surge in spending by increasing the prices of their products and services. They have no choice, as they can't physically produce more stuff. The result is inflation.

MMT critic Thomas Palley compares MMT's theory with an on/off switch.[3] If there is any level of slack, the inflation switch is in the "off" position, and increases in spending are matched by more production—one more dollar of spending is matched by one more dollar worth of new products. If there is no slack, the inflation switch is in the "on" position, and all increases in spending are matched by higher prices.

MMT's theory of inflation is extremely naive. Most economists think the relationship between spending and inflation is more complicated. They think a surge in spending can cause inflation *even if there is slack*.

There are many reasons why this may happen. One is that companies may respond to a surge in spending through a mix of more production and higher prices—even if they have spare capacity.[4] That happened in Rome after the Pope's death. Hotels increased their prices even if they were left with spare capacity—occupancy was 88% on the night of the funeral, not 100%.

Another reason is that different sectors in the economy have different levels of slack. Suppose the government increases its spending on building new houses. This endeavor requires a multitude of resources, including labor, materials, and machines. Perhaps some of these markets benefit from slack. For example, there may be unemployed workers in the labor market. But other markets may not benefit from slack. For example, the production of cement may already be running at full capacity. So, higher spending on house building ends up competing against the private sector's demand for cement, which causes the prices of cement to go up. It is very hard to guarantee that an increase in spending will *only* mobilize idle resources and won't interfere at all with the private sector.

In addition, many economists think that higher utilization of resources gives bargaining power to their owners, which causes price hikes. For example, if a bout of spending reduces unemployment, companies will find it harder to find new workers. This could give bargaining power to workers, who become able to negotiate pay raises. Companies end up passing some of the cost of higher wages to consumers, thus causing price hikes.

By the sounds of it, inflation is more like a dimmer switch, not an on/off switch. As spending increases around the economy, inflation is progressively activated. Inflation becomes active way before everyone has a job, every machine is turned on 24/7, and every material is used.

In recent times, some MMTers have started adding caveats to their original on/off theory, which aligns it a bit more to the views of mainstream economists. For example, Stephanie Kelton says:

> As an economy moves closer to its full employment limit, real resources become increasingly scarce. Rising demand can begin to put pressure on prices, and bottlenecks can develop in industries that are experiencing the greatest strain on capacity. Inflation can heat up. Once the economy hits this full employment wall, any additional spending (not just government spending) will be inflationary.[5]

William Mitchell adds:

> When the economy is operating at high pressure (high levels of capacity utilisation) workers are more able to secure money wage gains. This is especially the case if they are organised into coherent trade unions, which function as a countervailing force to the power of employers ... In a high pressure economy, firms may also initiate an inflationary process by trying to increase their profit margins.[6]

But MMTers quickly put these caveats aside. This is because they think there is currently a lot of slack in our economies. So, in practice, there is a lot of room to increase government spending with the switch still in the "off" position.

Let's see how MMT suggests increasing government spending—to exploit the available slack—while keeping inflation under control.

THE MMT WAY

MMTers think our economies have been running well below full capacity for a very long time. They often say that the existence of unemployment of any level proves economic resources are severely underutilized. Stephanie Kelton explains:

When we run our economy below its productive capacity, it means that we are living below our collective means. The federal budget might be in deficit, but we are underspending whenever there is unused capacity. It's like building a high-performance automobile and then driving it like it's a golf cart. It's inefficient. When we tolerate mass unemployment, we're sacrificing whatever might have been produced if we had harnessed the time and energy of those who wanted to work but were denied access to jobs.

MMTer Randall Wray explains, "Unemployment is sufficient evidence of this condition, so if there is unemployment it means government spending is too low (or taxes are too high)."[7] MMTer Yeva Nersisyan claims European economies are "probably operating 25 percent or more below full capacity. Even the US today has substantial excess capacity."[8] While she doesn't justify this figure, it seems to come from a pessimistic calculation of the unemployment rate, which is used as a proxy for of overall "slack."

So, MMT recommends, for starters, that the government increase its spending right away in order to exploit the unused capacity that is widely available around the economy. This additional spending should be funded by money creation instead of taxes. This way, government spending is increased without reducing private spending. So, total spending—public and private combined—goes up, and thus more unused resources are put to good use.

Government spending should go up until all productive capacity is exhausted. In particular, unemployment should go down to zero. If there's any level of unemployment, there is still room for more spending.

The increase in spending has no adverse consequences. In particular, it doesn't cause inflation, as only unused resources are mobilized, which is possible thanks to pervasive slack. MMTer Yeva Nersisyan explains:

> Below full employment, government spending creates "free lunches" as it utilizes resources that would otherwise be left idle.[9]

MMTers think we should stop obsessing about budgets. Instead, we should let the government keep spending more—and create money for it—provided that it can still mobilize increasingly more idle productive resources. Stephanie Kelton says:

> At its core, MMT is about replacing the (flawed) concept of a government budget constraint with a natural resource (inflation) constraint.[10]

But this isn't over yet. Once the economy runs at full capacity, the government must make sure nobody—private or public—tries to spend more. The economy is already at capacity, so any more spending will turn the inflation switch to the "on" position.

Suppose the government predicts that the private sector will get a bit too enthusiastic about a certain technology and will want to spend a lot on it—think of the wave of new AI start-ups launched after the release of ChatGPT. The government must preemptively increase taxes to cut down private spending. This way, it keeps total spending—public and private—at the exact amount needed to run the economy at full capacity. Alternatively, the government could reduce its own spending to offset the private surge in spending.

Suppose instead that the government, rather than the private sector, wants to spend more. For example, it may want to help insulate homes all around the country as part of an environmental initiative. Because the economy is already running at capacity, the government must increase taxes to suppress private spending and offset its additional spending. Stephanie Kelton explains:

> MMT would have us begin by asking if it would be safe for Congress to authorize $2 trillion in new spending without offsets. A careful analysis of the economy's existing (and anticipated) slack would guide lawmakers in making that determination ... Perhaps one-third, one-half, or three-fourths of the spending would need to be offset.

Remember, however, that in the MMT world, such a tax increase is not used to "fund" the government. It's simply used to liberate productive resources from the private sector and use them for public projects. MMTer Yeva Nersisyan explains:

> If taxes are to be used, they must be formulated to reduce resource use—not to "raise revenue."[11]

But what if the government miscalculates available resources or doesn't succeed in raising taxes to the exact level to control private spending? In this case, MMT suggests using an array of alternative measures to stymie price increases by law. MMTer Yeva Nersisyan explains:

> If inflation is likely, we need to put in place anti-inflationary measures, such as well-targeted taxes, wage and price controls, rationing, and voluntary saving.[12]

The MMT approach may sound seductive at first, but it suffers from numerous problems.

First, it is politically naive. It asks us to trust politicians—presumably MMTers—to raise taxes abruptly by just the right amount if they anticipate inflation. MMT critic Thomas Palley says, "The reality is taxes are politically contested and difficult to raise."[13] In addition, MMT assumes taxes can be modified rapidly and the effects of this on spending will kick in right away. This is hard to believe.[14] Moreover, trying to outlaw price increases, for example, through price controls, is known not to work very well in practice. It tends to result in empty shelves, not stable prices.

Second, MMT seems to consider workers to be the only resource needed for production and unemployment the only indicator of slack. In reality, projects require a variety of resources, such as workers, materials, and machines. Moreover, it's unlikely the government can satisfy its increased spending *only* by using idle resources. If it decides to, say, build a hospital, how can it guarantee it will only rely on unemployed workers, spare materials, and idle machines for the project? It is likely that, instead, the government's increased spending will compete against the private sector for some of the same resources, which will interfere with prices.

Third, MMT's recommended policy relies on the on/off model of inflation, despite MMTers' own caveats about it. As discussed earlier, this model doesn't seem quite right for many reasons. For example, many economists think that extremely low unemployment could give bargaining power to workers, which would lead to increased wages and prices. The inflation switch is "on" before all slack has been removed.

Fourth, MMT assumes there will be no changes in private behavior as a result of increased government spending. This is unrealistic. It is more likely that the private sector will analyze government's future intended actions and change its current spending patterns as a result, neutralizing the government's efforts.[15]

But there's an even bigger elephant in the room. MMT's policy adds progressively more money to the economy over time, as new money is constantly created to fund the increased and ongoing deficit. Year after year, people find themselves with increasingly more money in their bank accounts.

This doesn't sound like great news. If people have increasingly more money in their pockets, economists fear they will use it one day, and this will cause inflation. MMT critic Thomas Palley explains that money created by MMT-style deficits "embodies latent purchasing power." He adds that "even if not activated immediately on issue," this money "may be activated at a future date and it can be difficult to deactivate it in a nondisruptive fashion."[16]

MMT contests this point. It says putting progressively more money in people's pockets is not an issue. Some MMTers even deny this is what MMT recommends. Let's dig a bit deeper into that.

Inflation

AN EXPLOSION OF MONEY

The word on the street is that too much "money printing" can cause inflation. Suppose you give one million dollars of newly created money to every household. It is conceivable that they will at some point spend that money instead of putting it under the mattress and forgetting about it. As a result, prices will go up. In fact, prices may go up the moment this policy is announced, even before any money reaches anyone's pockets! This is because businesses will anticipate an imminent increase in purchasing power, and they will raise their prices ahead of time. If this weren't how things work, poverty could be easily resolved by giving one million dollars of newly printed money to each household.

MMT says that persistent money creation will not necessarily cause inflation because people love to hoard money. So, the newly created money will end up under the mattress, satisfying people's desire to save. In fact, MMTers have argued that the reason unemployment exists in the first place is that people want to save money instead of spending it.

MMTer Randall Wray explains:

> Unemployment is *de facto* evidence that the government's deficit is too low to provide the level of net saving desired ... In a sense, unemployment results because the government has kept the supply of fiat money too scarce.[17]

By creating progressively more money, the government will satisfy people's desire to save more. At the same time, the government's additional spending will increase employment and welfare, so it's "two birds, one shot." Randall Wray explains:

> If the private sector chronically desires to save more than it wants to invest, the government can fill the "demand gap" by deficit spending and thus allow households to save as much as desired ... At the same time, the additional deficit spending would increase incomes and generate additional spending, and thus additional employment.[18]

MMTers seem to believe the public has a never-ending desire to hoard money, so the government can keep creating more forever. For example, MMTer William Mitchell defines the MMT approach as "the use of continuous budget deficits in defence of full employment."[19] Despite what one may interpret from this comment, MMTers often deny they advocate money creation in itself. Instead, they say they advocate money creation only if it's necessary to respond to people's excessive money-hoarding habits.

So, what would happen if one day people stopped wanting to hoard progressively more money under the mattress? MMTer Éric Tymoigne assures us that, in that case, the government will reduce its deficit and stop creating more money to pay for it. In fact, this will happen automatically! This is because, if people start spending more, the economy will do better, and thus the government will collect more taxes. So, this will automatically eliminate any excess money that people don't want to hoard. Tymoigne explains:

> There is no need to proactively raise taxes (i.e., raise tax rates or impose new taxes) and cut spending as the economy does better if strong enough automatic stabilizers are in place ... Automatic stabilizers will move the fiscal balance to the level desired by the nonfederal sector ... At this point, the fiscal balance is neither too high, nor too low, but rather accommodates the needs of the economy.[20]

Tymoigne also believes that the banking system will automatically wipe out money that people don't want to hoard. This is because, if people find themselves with too much spare cash, they will repay their loans and mortgages, so their savings will end up being absorbed by the banking system instead of circulating and causing inflation.[21]

There are many problems with MMT's views. First, its assumptions about money-hoarding seem implausible. MMT assumes that the private sector wants to hoard an ever-increasing total amount of money. For example, in year one, a business chooses to save 10% of its revenue, in year two, it chooses to save *another* 10%, and so on. If so, the business grows a larger and larger stash of savings over time. By year 10, the business will probably have accumulated savings above 100% of its yearly revenue.

If this were the case, the government could indeed *constantly* create new money, year after year, without causing inflation. The new money would simply offset the money that has gone under the mattress.

But that's not how it works. People and businesses like to have *some* savings. However, once they accumulate a minimum desired level of savings, they do not usually want to continue saving at a large rate every year, topping up and topping up the stash. MMT critic Thomas Palley says MMT assumes "implausible conditions" about people's demand for money.[22]

Second, the connection between money-hoarding and unemployment isn't clear. MMT assumes that, because companies want to hoard money, they decide not to hire more people. But why is that so? Suppose companies decided not to save money. Would that mean the economy would run exactly at full capacity, with every machine turned on and unemployment at zero? If so, why? There seems to be a missing theoretical link between the different concepts.

Third, MMTers ask us to believe that automatic mechanisms will guarantee that the amount of newly created money will correspond *exactly* to the amount of extra money the public wants under the mattress—not more, not less. This is hard to believe, as it would require an extremely well calibrated tax and banking system. Note that MMTers also contradict themselves on this point, as they often say taxes should be actively used to dampen inflation.

Fourth, increasing the amount of money in people's hands may lower the value of the local currency in foreign exchange markets. This is because some people may convert that money into other currencies. This makes imports more expensive and can cause inflation locally. This mechanism has been the source of much criticism against MMT.

MMTers have responded to this criticism. They've suggested that the government could prevent this by fixing the value of its currency against the value of a foreign currency. For example, the government could establish a band within which exchange rates are allowed to fluctuate.[23] But this only works if the government accumulates enough reserves of foreign currency so that it can dump it into the market to affect exchange rates whenever this is needed. In this case, the government must budget "the household way" to amass enough foreign currency, as it cannot create foreign currency. This contradicts the rest of MMT, which assumes the government doesn't promise to convert the national currency against anything else for any predetermined exchange rate. This policy suggestion undermines monetary sovereignty, which MMT has been advocating for years.

Let's now turn to history. Let's see how MMT explains past episodes of inflation, from the tame and persistent inflation in the United States since the late 1980s, to the dramatic hyperinflation in Zimbabwe.

WHAT ABOUT THE PRICE OF EGGS?

Inflation has been persistent in many places around the world for decades. In the United States, for example, prices have multiplied by a factor of eight since the 1960s. Even during the calm period going from 1985 to 2019, in which inflation was low compared to other periods, prices were multiplied by a factor of two.

MMT says that the United States and most countries have been severely *underutilizing* their resources—slack is endemic. The proof of this is the existence of unemployment. But, according to MMT's own theory, then there shouldn't be inflation! If you remember, the inflation switch is in the "off" position whenever there is slack. So how can MMT explain that inflation has occurred even in the presence of slack?

MMT has a couple of answers to this conundrum. According to MMTer Randall Wray, the problem is that the calculation of inflation is inaccurate. In particular, the consumer price index, or CPI, which is used to measure the price of products around the economy, overestimates price increases. He explains:

> To measure price changes, we must compare prices in one year—a base year—with prices in later (and earlier) years. This is much harder than it sounds, because not only do prices change, but products and services change, too. We must adjust the CPI or other measures of price for quality improvements. How much would a modern laptop have cost in 1966? ... The CPI is more of an art than a science since we have to put prices on things that did not exist and make hard to quantify quality adjustments. So, yes, the price of a new car today is more than ten times higher than it was in 1974, but it is also much more sophisticated, safer, and more comfortable.[24]

This seems a bit exaggerated, however. The US Bureau of Labor Statistics, which calculates the CPI, uses several methods to adjust the CPI for quality improvements. Its website explains:

> Hedonic quality adjustment is one of the techniques the CPI uses to account for changing product quality within some CPI item samples ... The CPI uses hedonic quality adjustments in item categories that tend to experience a high degree of quality change either due to seasonal changes, as in apparel items, or because of innovative improvements and technological changes, as in consumer appliances and electronics.[25]

While this method may not be perfect—and it's been criticized by many people—it's hard to conclude that persistent inflation in the United States is *only* the result of a measurement error. I'm pretty sure shoppers wouldn't agree. Some Americans may recall a dozen eggs used to cost 75 cents in 1985. They'd be lucky now to buy a dozen eggs for three times that price.[26] Similarly, some British shoppers may recall a dozen eggs used to cost 80 pence in 1985.[27] Now the price is two and a half times higher. Could that be down to an impressive increase in the quality of eggs?

Note that another popular price index, known as the PCE index, also shows that there has been persistent inflation over time in the United States. This index is more comprehensive that the CPI, as it covers more products, and it adapts more quickly to changes in consumer behavior. Could the PCE index also be so inaccurately calculated that it generates the illusion of inflation?

Randall Wray also proposes an alternative explanation for persistent inflation. Over time, different sectors of the economy increase their productivity at different rates, so their relative prices of products and services vary over time. This is known as the Baumol effect. Wray thinks this effect can explain the apparent inflation in the United States. He explains:

> A symphony orchestra back in Mozart's time was as large as one today, give or take a few performers, and it took about the same time to perform a piece, depending on the conductor. There has been virtually no productivity improvement (same number of "workers" working the same number of hours to perform a symphony) ... There is a similar problem in many other areas, mostly services where you really cannot improve productivity much (think barbers, teachers, doctors) ...
>
> Blame the concert violinist for erosion of the value of the Dollar! In a sense, a part of inflation is to even these things out, otherwise all our musicians and artists would live like paupers relative to our factory workers. Think of it this way: inflation is the cost of preserving culture.[28]

There is a problem with this explanation though. It is true that the prices of some services have become relatively high compared to others. For example, a haircut may now cost the same as a short-haul flight on a low-cost airline. But productivity differences across sectors only explain changes in *relative* prices. They don't say much about in which direction all prices move and why prices have increased in general across all categories.[29]

Wray concludes:

> In sum, prices have trended upward for a variety of reasons. Some price rises have to do with measurement issues; some with Baumol disease.[30]

I'm pretty sure people who've been buying eggs over the years will not be convinced.

HYPERINFLATION AND HYPERVENTILATION

After the end of World War I, four countries—Austria, Hungary, Germany, and Poland—experienced dramatic inflation. Between 1921 and 1924, prices in Austria were multiplied by 242, in Hungary by 532, and in Poland by 9,639. The most extreme case was that of Germany, where prices were multiplied by 91 billion, to the point that ordinary purchases cost trillions of German marks.[31] In 1924, Germany introduced a new currency, which was declared equivalent to one trillion units of the previous one. This wiped out 12 zeros from banknotes, which I'm sure people found more convenient. The German episode became a textbook example of *hyperinflation*, which is usually defined as inflation so severe that prices go up by 50% or more in a single month.

After the war, the governments of Austria, Hungary, Germany, and Poland started creating a lot of money to pay their bills. For example, the Austrian government funded 40-67% of its spending by creating new money, depending on the year. In Germany, 52-88% of government spending was funded that way after the war. This was done indirectly, by asking the central bank to give the government ever-increasing "loans" funded by the creation of new money.

The reasons for so much money creation were varied. Austria, Hungary, and Germany had to pay expensive war reparations to their neighbors.

But it was politically difficult to increase taxes by a high-enough amount to pay them, especially right after such a devastating war. So, the governments of these countries resorted to money creation instead.

In addition, governments increased their spending to help the population recover from the war. For example, the government provided food relief and gave transfers to the unemployed. This made government spending higher and, once again, increasing taxes to pay for it was complicated, so money creation was used instead.

Moreover, as inflation soared, tax collection became ineffective. By the time an agreed amount of tax was collected, prices had gone up, so the government couldn't afford to do as much with that money as intended. So, the government topped up its accounts with more newly created money to make up for the loss of taxes' purchasing power.

To top it off, central banks provided highly subsidized loans to the private sector, which was facilitated by money creation.

As inflation picked up, the public started liking the national currency less and less and thus wanted to get rid of it faster and faster. This pushed prices even higher, as people tried to spend away their money as quickly as possible. This made the already high inflation even higher, transforming it into full-on hyperinflation.

The total amount of money in circulation increased dramatically during this period. For example, in Austria, it was multiplied by a factor of 288 in three years. In the more extreme case of Germany, it was multiplied by 5,748 in a period of 18 months. At one point, 90% of German banknotes in existence had been created in the previous 30 days.

Hyperinflation stopped abruptly in these four countries. Have a look at the graph on the next page, and you'll see prices flatline suddenly.[32]

In each of these four countries, inflation stopped abruptly the moment the government announced a credible plan to reduce government deficits and to stop the practice of creating money to pay for government spending. Economist Thomas Sargent explains that, in Austria,

Inflation

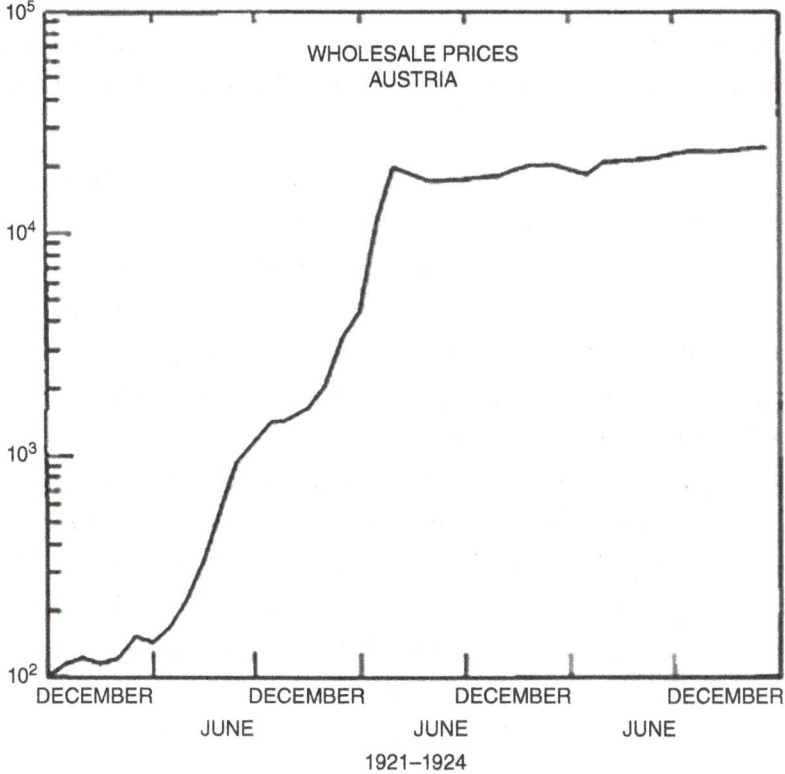

Source: [32]/with permission of National Bureau of Economic Research

... expenditures were reduced by discharging thousands of government employees. Under the reconstruction scheme, the government promised gradually to discharge a total of 100,000 state employees. Deficits in government enterprises were reduced by raising prices of government-sold goods and services. New taxes and more efficient means of collecting tax and custom revenues were instituted ... Within two years the government was able to balance the budget.[33]

In Germany, the measures were similar. In 1925, economist John Park Young recorded the German experience as follows:

The number of government employees was cut by 25 percent; all temporary employees were to be discharged; all above the age of 65 years were to be retired. An additional 10 percent of the civil servants were to be discharged by January 1924. The railways, overstaffed as a result of post-war demobilization, discharged 120,000 men during 1923 and 60,000 more during 1924.[34]

Hungary and Poland also took actions to balance their budgets. In addition, the three countries that owed reparations renegotiated the terms of their debts, which was crucial to help them balance their budgets.

Moreover, the governments of the four countries established independent central banks that were highly limited or forbidden to lend money to the government. This gave the public confidence that money creation to fund the government would end.

But there's something even more staggering about the abrupt end of these inflations: They all ended right after the listed measures were *announced*, even though they hadn't been executed yet. This was likely because the public became confident that the oncoming reforms would work, so they stopped trying to get rid of government money as soon as they could. This stabilized prices ahead of time.

Economist think multiple factors contributed to inflation in these countries, such as the collapse of productive capacity—which pushed up prices of goods—and currency devaluation—which made imports more expensive. However, most agree that the creation of money to fund government spending played a crucial role—it either directly caused, amplified, or perpetuated inflation, and it may have been pivotal in turning it into hyperinflation. This becomes quite evident when we consider that inflation stopped just when it was announced that the practice of government funding by money creation would come to an end.

Another textbook example of hyperinflation was the one suffered by Zimbabwe between 2007 and 2009. The problem started to brew in 1997, when the government decided to grant 60,000 war veterans a one-off payment of 50,000 Zimbabwean dollars each (equivalent to 3,000 US dollars at the time) plus an ongoing monthly pension. This increased the government deficit by 55% that year alone. Initially, the government planned to raise a tax to pay for it, but then it gave up on this idea due to countrywide protests. Instead, the government resorted to money creation.[35]

Four months later, the president announced a drastic plan to redistribute farming land across the country, as the existing distribution was considered deeply unfair. For this, the government would acquire wide swathes of commercial farms, but it didn't explain how it would pay for them. As a result, international markets lost faith in the Zimbabwean dollar, as people suspected the land reform could cause all sorts of problems, and they doubted the government had a credible plan to fund it. The Zimbabwean dollar depreciated as a consequence. This made imports more expensive for the local population, which increased prices by 25% in a single month.

The government tried to implement price controls to limit price increases. This didn't work well—it resulted in a shortage of basic products in official markets and the growth of black markets.

Things became much more dramatic in 2000, when the government announced it would fast-track its land reform plan. The government would acquire thousands of farms for redistribution, but it wouldn't compensate the owners. An association of war veterans started occupying the soon-to-be-acquired land, which led to violent confrontations.[36] These events caused the collapse of agricultural production around the country. The lack of production intensified inflation. Prices went up at a rate of 100–600% over the next couple of years.

Economists think that, up to this point, a combination of money creation, pricier imports, and the drop in production were the culprits of high inflation. But the worst was yet to come.

In 2004, the Zimbabwean central bank started sowing the seeds of hyperinflation. To help restore the damaged agricultural sector, the bank started subsidizing producers with newly created money. For example, it gave a fixed subsidy to farmers for every kilogram of tobacco and cotton they produced. In addition, the central bank subsidized the purchase of foreign currency, further increasing money creation. These measures caused an explosion in the amount of money in existence. In 2006 alone, it increased by more than 1,000%.

In 2007, hyperinflation broke out as people tried to spend away the rapidly inflating currency. Prices multiplied by a factor of 41 in that year alone.[37] The central bank accelerated the pace of money creation, which reached 66,000% in 2007.[38]

Inflation accelerated even further in 2008. Prices multiplied by a factor of 25,337 from January to July that year.[39] A few months later, the central bank started issuing banknotes with a face value of one hundred trillion Zimbabwean dollars.

At this point, Zimbabweans pretty much dodged the national currency altogether and started using foreign currency for their transactions, which was illegal at the time. In January 2009, the government made it legal to use the US dollar and the South African rand for transactions. Prices stabilized afterward. Since then, Zimbabwe hasn't succeeded in reintroducing a stable national currency.

The link between money creation and hyperinflation has left many people uneasy about MMT. They think that, based on these past experiences, MMT could be a recipe for disaster.

MMTers tell us not to worry about that. To calm the waters, they've taken the time to analyze the hyperinflations of Germany and Zimbabwe and shared their findings.

In their analysis, MMTers acknowledge the role of government deficits—funded by money creation—in fueling hyperinflation in both cases. MMTer William Mitchell says, "In these circumstances, we do observe rising fiscal deficits … It is likely that tighter fiscal policy would have helped to reduce inflationary pressures."[40]

However, they say we shouldn't focus on the deficits themselves to analyze these episodes. Instead, we should focus on the situations that caused the deficits in the first place, which were "not normal."[41]

William Mitchell explains that reparation payments were one of the main causes for high deficits in Germany, as the government thought it was "politically impossible to raise taxes to a sufficient level … to pay the reparations. Instead it relied on spending in excess of taxes."[42] In addition, he argues that the productive capacity of the economy had been dramatically reduced due to war-related devastation. As a result, "government competed with domestic demand for a limited supply of output, thereby driving up prices."[43]

According to Mitchell, the Zimbabwean deficit was triggered by the disruption in agricultural production, itself caused by the land reform. He explains:

> The collapse in the supply side of the Zimbabwean economy explains the hyperinflation that followed. To avoid the hyperinflation, given the supply side contraction, the Zimbabwean government would have had to severely contract real spending to match the new lower capacity. Had the government implemented austerity to this degree, widespread starvation and deaths would have followed.[44]

Mitchell then adds:

> There are many paths to hyperinflation, but there are common problems: social and political upheaval, civil war, the collapse of productive capacity that could be due to war, weak government, and foreign debt denominated in an external currency or gold.[45]

MMTer Éric Tymoigne adds that "MMT rejects monetary sources of hyperinflation and focuses on the underlying productive, financial, and political instabilities."[46]

Because these situations were highly unusual, MMTers think they don't undermine MMT. This is because MMT's policies are meant to be applied in normal times by wise governments. William Mitchell concludes:

> So hyperventilate as you like but Zimbabwe does not make a case against the use of continuous budget deficits in defence of full employment.

Bad Governments will wreck any economy if they want to.

A wise government using the fiscal capacity provided to it by a fiat monetary system can engender full employment and equity yet also sustain price stability.[47]

I find these explanations a bit hard to navigate. On the one hand, they tell us that deficits—funded by money creation—did contribute to hyperinflation. On the other hand, they tell us these deficits were "not normal," so they don't really count. But does it matter whether the deficits were normal or not? I think most people fear that an MMT-style government will create too much money and cause an inflation problem, even if this is done during "normal" times when peace prevails and farms operate just fine.

In addition, MMTers seem to imply that, while the government should be allowed to create money, we should make sure a "wise" government is put in charge of it—perhaps one led by, say, MMTer William Mitchell himself. I'm not sure this will calm down hyperventilators.

THE COVID-19 EXPERIMENT

In 2020, economies around the world ground to a halt due to pandemic-related lockdowns. Many governments took dramatic measures to stimulate the economy. This included paying for people's wages in the private sector—even if they weren't working—and handing out checks to the population. In the United States, the government stimulus package was the largest in its history. It included handing $1,200 checks to millions of households in March 2020, topped up by an additional $600 in December 2020, and a further $1,400 in March 2021. Over 150 million households received such transfers.[48] In the United Kingdom, the government paid 80% of the salary of 11.7 million private-sector employees whose jobs had been affected by lockdowns.[49]

To fund these measures, governments issued bonds in order to borrow money from the public. However, central banks simultaneously created new money and bought the bonds on resale. As discussed in the previous chapter, many people think this meant that the COVID-19 stimulus was effectively funded by money creation, just like MMT would have recommended. Because of this, MMT was put on the spotlight at the time. Some people even claimed, "We are all MMTers now."

MMTers celebrated stimulus packages. MMTer Stephanie Kelton supported the packages and claimed, "It took a virus to kill the deficit myth."[50] This was perhaps the greatest victory lap in MMT's history.

Some MMTers were careful enough to clarify that "helicopter drops of cash" were not exactly what MMT recommended, but they welcomed the development. In fact, they claimed this taught us that the government could have been doing this kind of thing earlier, even before the pandemic hit. MMTer Yeva Nersisyan says:

> Those invoking MMT misrepresent its main tenets … What we emphasize is that sovereign governments face resource constraints, not financial constraints … Unemployment is evidence that the country is living below its means … An important lesson to learn from the COVID-19 crisis is that the government's ability to run deficits is not limited to times of crisis. Indeed, it was a policy error to keep the economy below full employment before this crisis hit.[51]

MMTers didn't worry about the stimulus packages, which they thought wouldn't cause inflation. In February 2021, right before the last round of checks were sent out in the United States, Yeva Nersisyan explained:

> The propensity to consume out of these checks will not be high, as most people will use them to pay down debts or replenish savings (only 29 percent of the first round of checks was spent on consumption, while 34 percent was used to pay down debt and the rest was saved). What little boost to consumption they will provide can be handled without inflation, as production around the world has rebounded sufficiently.[52]

A few months later, in mid-2021, inflation soared around the world. Countries like the United States and the United Kingdom found themselves with inflation rates they hadn't experienced in decades, often reaching double figures.

MMTers don't think this bout of inflation had much to do with MMT. Stephanie Kelton explains:

> So here's what the so-called "MMT experiment" has shown: (1) The mechanics of government finance work precisely the way MMT has always described. (2) The federal government is not revenue constrained. (3) There was no need to raise taxes in order to finance trillions in new spending ...
>
> There was, however, a big move up in inflation following the passage of the March 2021 fiscal package. And this has led some people to ask whether the emergence of high inflation means that the MMT experiment has failed. The answer is an unequivocal no.
>
> Why?
>
> Because MMT offers a descriptive framework—a lens—through which to evaluate fiscal and monetary policy. MMT did not urge the Fed to do $120 billion in asset purchases every month. MMT did not write the $2.2T CARES Act. It did not advise Congress to launch the payroll protection program, to send out $1,200 checks or to provide $600/week in federal unemployment compensation. A *framework* cannot do those things ...
>
> The point is, you can't blame "MMT" for stoking inflation any more than you can blame an optometrist if her patient runs off the road while driving without wearing their prescription lenses.[53]

The exact causes of 2021s bout of inflation are disputed. Some economists believe it was due to pandemic-related supply chain disruption and later intensified by the war in Ukraine. MMTers endorse this explanation. For example, Randall Wray says:

> Beyond pandemic-related disruptions, the Ukrainian war also affects energy and food supplies, and thus prices. Also important, although less so, are weather-related impacts on production (especially of food) related to global climate change.[54]

Stephanie Kelton adds:

> We need a unified and coordinated push to bring down the price of oil, which is the major driver of inflation, not just here in the U.S. but across much of the world ... First and foremost, we need a negotiated resolution to the war in Ukraine ... And keep working to reduce costs for families who are struggling with high food and energy. All of these (and more) are good ideas: Lower the cost of prescription drugs; ... Deal with known cases of price gouging; ... Build housing![55]

But many economists remain unconvinced of this explanation. They think that supply chain disruptions and oil prices may have had *something* to do with inflation initially, but they don't tell us the full story. They think that government stimulus packages, facilitated by money creation, fueled inflation.

According to this view, government stimulus caused overly high consumer spending. Much of this spending kicked in with a delay, as people could only go out and spend money once lockdowns were lifted. Moreover, some economists think stimulus facilitated high demand for labor, which caused an increase in wages and amplified inflation.

Ben Bernanke, the former chairman of the US Federal Reserve, explains that there were

> ... increases in overall consumer spending driven by supportive monetary and fiscal policies ... The combination of an increased demand for goods and limited supply resulted, not surprisingly, in sharp rises in prices in a number of sectors ...
>
> As many have recognized, the inflation largely reflected strong aggregate demand, the product of easy fiscal and monetary policies, excess savings accumulated during the pandemic, and the reopening of locked-down economies. The strength of aggregate demand led to a (belatedly recognized) tightening of the labor market, as reflected in record high ratios of job openings to unemployed workers.[56]

Economic advisor Stephen D. King adds:

> Yes, inflation would have been lower had Russia not invaded Ukraine. It would not, however, easily have returned to "target" ... The stock of money had risen hugely in a relatively short space of time. And, for much of that time, people were unable to spend, owing to the effects of lockdowns ... As lockdowns ended, money velocity picked up: suddenly, the earlier increase in what had been "idle" money balances could be put to good use.[57]

Former Bank of England governor Mervyn King put it more bluntly:

> They shouldn't have been printing the extra money ... You know, if we keep printing money at this rate, what will happen? And the answer is obvious: you'll get inflation.[58]

THE LATIN AMERICAN EXPERIMENT

Since the 1970s, many Latin American countries have suffered from repeated episodes of high inflation or even hyperinflation.

The most recent episodes took place in Venezuela and Argentina. Venezuela started suffering from three-digit inflation in 2015, when the rate of price increases reached 120%. Hyperinflation broke out in 2018, when the rate of price increases surpassed 63,000%. The inflation rate remains in the double or triple digits as of this writing.[59] In Argentina, inflation reached double digits in 2007, and it reached a peak of 211% in 2023.[60]

Economists and politicians often explain Latin American inflation by focusing on unfortunate external triggers. These triggers lead to a chain of events that result in inflation. For example, you'll hear that, in 2018, the United States increased interest rates, which made US investments more attractive to international investors. This caused international investors to pull money away from Argentina and move into the United States. As a result, the value of the Argentina peso depreciated in international markets. This made imports more expensive for Argentineans, which increased inflation. In addition, Argentinean farms suffered from a devastating drought, which compounded the problem.

According to these explanations, every inflationary episode in Latin America is different, and they're all very unfortunate and outside of the government's control. Perhaps there's some truth to it, but it makes one wonder whether there's more to the story. One of my friends lost his passport four times within two years. He has a perfectly reasonable explanation for each of these events—and it was never his fault. But it makes one wonder if he's just not very careful with his passport.

Many economists think there are deeper explanations of Latin American inflation other that the individual, external triggers that are often mentioned.

One common explanation is as follows. During periods of discontent, Latin American governments have a tendency to widely expand their scope and increase their spending to help the population. The government does this in numerous ways, such as building social housing, increasing transfers to families with young children, and nationalizing and subsidizing poorly performing companies.

The government even gets pretty creative at times. For example, when I was a teenager in Argentina, the government handed out free laptops to young students across the country, as part of a program called "connected equality." Between 2010 and 2015, a total of five million laptops were provided, which covered 10% of the country's population.[61]

The government doesn't worry too much about the consequences of its expansion. It often justifies it using a rhetoric that is very similar to MMT. For example, it argues that there is plenty of slack in the economy, which can absorb the additional spending. Americo Zorrilla, the Chilean minister of finance in the 1970s, explained:

> The subutilization of installed capacity is another feature of the current economic situation ... In 1969 it was possible to increase production, due to subutilization, by more than 30 percent ... According to recent studies ... unutilized capacity has reached, in the last few years, 61 percent in the cloth industry, 50 percent in the baking industry ... 74 percent in the shoe industry, etc.[62]

Economist Sergio Bitar, who was minister of mining at the time, explained:

> Since there was a substantial margin for expanding supply, it was concluded that the increase in demand would not provoke an acceleration of inflation.[63]

Chile ended up with inflation above 500% in the 1970s.

More recently, in 2019, soon-to-become Argentine president Alberto Fernandez explained:

> The great deficit is that Argentina's economy has turned off. We need to reignite industry, make closed shops reopen their doors, make machines function, fill factories with workers who produce and export goods.[64]

Inflation soared during Fernandez' mandate.

In some cases, Latin American governments fund their expansions through money creation right away.[65] In other cases, this happens in a more subtle way. First, the government expands during a period of bonanza, in which its revenue from tax collection and other sources is high. However, Latin American governments have a tendency not to adapt their budgeting afterward, when circumstances change. Instead, if there's a shock that affects their revenue or spending, they will top up their accounts by creating money.

This is how things went in the recent episodes of high inflation in Argentina and Venezuela. The government first expanded when its revenue was high. In Venezuela, the price of oil was high, so government revenue from oil was favorable. In Argentina, the prices of agricultural exports were high, so tax collection from farming was significant.

When the oil price came down, the Venezuelan government maintained its fiscal generosity despite reduced revenue, and it made up for the difference by creating money. The government kept expanding afterward despite the drop in revenue. Such was the case that, when the price of oil went back up, the government still had to create money to keep up with its ever-increasing spending. Something similar happened in Argentina. When tax collection from agricultural exports dropped, the government kept up its generous spending and used money creation to pay for it.

An aggravating factor is that many Latin American countries have accumulated a lot of external debt, which they owe to other countries in foreign currency. Unfortunate events can make this debt more expensive to pay. For example, the local currency may depreciate, making it more expensive to obtain the foreign currency required to pay the debt. Instead of increasing taxes, which would be politically unpopular, the government resorts to money creation to service the debt, much like Germany in the 1920s. Note, however, that it is hard to blame Latin American inflation solely on this effect, as there have been notorious episodes of high inflation in which external debt was small.[66]

Economist Rudiger Dornbusch studied episodes of extreme inflation in Latin America. He concluded that inflation was indeed triggered by shocks, including "a major shock to the budget, the terms of trade, or the exchange rate."[67] However, what turned the shocks into extreme inflation was that, in response to them, the government automatically created as much money as needed to maintain its level of spending.

Economist Stanley Fischer adds:

The sensitivity of the inflation rate to small shocks probably results from holding the deficit constant and working with seigniorage [which means money creation] as the residual source of financing.[68]

A group of economists studied the economic history of 11 Latin American countries from 1960 to 2017.[69] They concluded that the common denominator of Latin American inflation was a lack of fiscal discipline. Latin American governments seem a little too willing to spend in excess of revenue and top up their accounts with newly created money.

Economist Sebastian Edwards thinks Latin American–style budgeting may be interpreted as a sort of MMT experiment. He explains:

> It turns out that MMT—or some version of it—has been tried in a number of emerging countries ... Almost every one of the Latin American experiments with major central bank-financed fiscal expansions took place under populist regimes, and all of them ended up badly, with runaway inflation, huge currency devaluations, and precipitous real wage declines. In most of these episodes—Argentina, Bolivia, Brazil, Chile, Ecuador, Nicaragua, Peru, and Venezuela—policymakers used arguments similar to those made by MMTers to justify extensive use of money creation to finance very large increases in public expenditures.[70]

But MMT supporters don't quite agree. They say, "Real Modern Monetary Theory has never been tried."[71]

WHY DOES INFLATION MATTER?

Prices go up. So what? Suppose prices go up by 10%. Let's assume for a minute that wages also go up by 10%. At the end of the day, your real purchasing power doesn't change, as you can still afford the same amount of stuff with your updated wage. In this case, we can think of inflation as a change of units, such as switching a speed limit from miles per hour to its equivalent in kilometers per hour. The numbers get larger, but the underlying reality does not.

Most economists don't think this is how it works. They think inflation can have multiple negative effects, including harming economic performance in the long run.

One of the reasons for this is that high inflation makes it difficult for businesses and households to plan ahead.[72] So, people become reluctant to enter long-term contracts such as loans. For example, in Argentina, mortgages are virtually nonexistent. If you want to buy a house, you must save the entire amount in US dollar bills. Banks fear they won't be able to predict inflation rates accurately and set interest rates accordingly, so they'd rather not offer mortgages at all. Economist Filipe Campante explains, "The disappearance of long term contracts has a negative impact on productivity."[73]

In addition, economists think inflation messes up the pricing system, as prices adjust at different speeds across the economy. This causes distortions that make economic decisions inefficient, which causes long-term harm.[74]

The Bank of England summarizes these points as follows: "If inflation is too high or it moves around a lot, it's hard for businesses to set the right prices and for people to plan their spending."[75]

Inflation also causes political problems. For starters, it acts like a stealthy tax paid by anyone with spare money. You can think of this as follows: You're charged a tax in exchange for the privilege of holding money. If you hold money too long, it will be worth less and less over time, as you're constantly being taxed for holding it. Note that this a "regressive" tax, as it affects poorer people the most. Poorer people hold a larger portion of their wealth in the form of money, as they must use it quickly to pay the bills. On the contrary, richer people hold most of their wealth in the form of revenue-generating assets like real estate, which isn't affected by the "inflation tax" in the way money does.

Another political problem is that wages don't always rise as fast as prices. So, workers become frustrated because their purchasing power is eroded over time. To top it off, workers are often pushed to higher tax brackets because their wages rise but the boundaries of the brackets are not updated quickly enough. Pensioners also suffer, as their income often struggles to keep up with inflation.

As a result of the economic and political problems caused by inflation, most economists think inflation is bad news, and central banks try to take actions to keep inflation low and stable. They usually target a 2% inflation rate a year, which is seen as 0% inflation plus a margin of safety to avoid deflation.

MMTers don't seem to worry too much about inflation, or they seem to think it's preferable to other outcomes. For example, Stephanie Kelton says, "You know what is worse than inflation? A crawling recovery."[76]

In their 500-page textbook on macroeconomics, MMTer William Mitchell and his colleagues don't mention any possible negative effects of inflation.[77] This contrasts with most macroeconomics textbooks, which dedicate at least a few pages to the topic.[78]

Moreover, MMTers seem to believe that fear of inflation is unfounded. MMTer Randall Wray explains:

> There isn't much evidence that low but persistent inflation actually harms economic performance, although people do not like it.[79]

My impression is that this statement results from an overly narrow interpretation of the existing evidence. Many studies have shown that inflation, even at a low or moderate level, does impact long-term economic performance in a negative way.[80] There is some controversy, however, because a minority of studies have found no such relationship. It's hard to conclude from all this that low inflation is harmless. Economist Otmar Issing explains:

> While some controversy remains, it is fair to say that the weight of the evidence does point to a negative relationship between inflation and output in the long run. That is, inflation is bad for growth in the long run. A number of such studies have been carried out, mainly looking at the experiences of groups of countries over extended periods …

The result is not unanimous, however. McCandless and Weber (1995), for example, reach the conclusion that there is no correlation between growth and inflation. However, no study of which I am aware manages to find a positive relation ... A recent study by Andrés and Hernando (1999), focusing on the countries of the Organisation for Economic Co-operation and Development (OECD), finds that even in low- or moderate-inflation countries, there is evidence of a robust negative relationship between inflation and output in the long run.[81]

Overall, most economists conclude that inflation is bad news due to the preponderance of empirical evidence against it, coupled with theoretical and political reasons to avoid it.

In addition, economists are afraid inflation could be a slippery slope—once it kicks in, it's hard to stop, and it gets increasingly worse. MMTers tell us not to worry about that. Randall Wray says:

> Let us turn to much higher inflation rates, which do harm economies. We will see that extremely high inflation is unusual. Further, there appears to be no reason to believe that the sort of "creeping" inflation that is common will gradually rise to hyperinflationary rates.

High inflation has indeed been relatively uncommon in the countries typically studied by MMT. But why is that so? Hyperventilators may fear it's been uncommon precisely because politicians haven't been allowed to create money in the way MMTers want.

FINAL THOUGHTS

Stephanie Kelton says:

> The Fed has no reliable theory of inflation guiding its day-to-day decision-making. It has various conjectures, assumptions, and models, but many of these are unproven or indeed unprovable. It's all something of a guessing game, where people's lives are on the line.[82]

I'll just add one thing: Where exactly is MMT's reliable theory of inflation? I haven't found it. This chapter has shown that its theory is rather unconvincing.

If you're interested, Appendix D contains further comments about inflation. It includes a discussion of how central banks fight inflation today, and why MMTers dislike it. It also includes a discussion of the recent steep drop of inflation in Argentina, under Javier Milei's "chainsaw" policy. As this an ongoing development—and we don't know how it will unfold—I thought it was better left to the appendix for now.

In the next chapter, we turn to the topic of unemployment. Economists have been debating for nearly 100 years why unemployment exists and why it persists. MMT makes fighting unemployment its topmost priority, and it offers a clear-cut explanation for its causes, as well as a definitive solution. Let's see.

CHAPTER FIVE

UNEMPLOYMENT, AND HOW TO FIX IT

My uncle was struggling to sell his house. He told me that the reason for it was, "People just aren't buying houses." I asked him, "What is your asking price? Could it be that it's too high, and that's why no one's buying it?" He answered, "No. The price has nothing to do with it. In this terrible market, people just aren't buying houses."

I wasn't convinced. I thought of replying, "I will buy your house for one dollar."

When something remains unsold, it is tempting to argue that "people aren't buying." However, economists don't like this kind of explanation. They think there are deeper reasons for people not buying, and they like to study them. For example, they often investigate market frictions that could leave things unsold, such as an overly high price, a complicated search process, an overly rigid contract, and so on. Could it be that my uncle's asking price was too high? Could it be that he was listing the house in the wrong place?

Let's now turn to the topic of unemployment. Being unemployed means you're willing and able to work but haven't yet been able to find a job. We can think of unemployment as labor remaining unsold, just like my uncle's house.

We often hear that the reason for unemployment is that "there aren't enough jobs." This is similar to "people just aren't buying houses." Once again, economists don't usually like this type of explanation, as it doesn't get to the bottom of the issue. Instead, they prefer studying deeper reasons for unemployment and its persistence over time, such as market frictions.

The oldest and most trivial explanation is that unemployment is caused by wages being rigid—they tend not to adapt to circumstances and often remain too high. This can be due to minimum-wage laws, union actions, or even societal norms. Suppose there's a crisis, say, the collapse of the housing market or the burst of a technology bubble. If wages don't go down to compensate for this, some labor may remain unsold, just like my uncle's house. According to this view, a drop in wages may sometimes be necessary to reduce unemployment, which makes this explanation for unemployment politically unpopular.

A more modern explanation is that the job search process is inefficient at matching candidates with relevant jobs. This is because jobs are very different from one another and require special skills. When there's a crisis in one sector, such as housing, it takes time to match workers to new jobs that require different skills. The result is unemployment.

Another popular explanation is that companies tend to pay unnecessarily high wages to motivate employees, as they're afraid workers won't do their best jobs otherwise. This leaves some people unemployed, as companies prefer to hire a lower number of motivated employees than a higher number of unmotivated ones.

Yet another explanation is that work contracts tend to be too long and inflexible. Businesses are unwilling to commit long term, due to uncertainty about the future, and this causes unemployment.

Although progress has been made, economists haven't yet agreed on a conclusive explanation for unemployment. Some think it's a mix of the things I've just mentioned.[1] Unemployment is perhaps one of the greatest unsolved problems in economics. Because it isn't completely understood, it's also hard to fight it—you'll hear different economists propose different solutions.

MMT endorses one specific explanation for unemployment, which was formulated by economist John Maynard Keynes in the 1930s. We will cover it in the first half of this chapter. MMT also proposes one specific policy to completely eliminate unemployment. This policy, known as a job guarantee, is MMT's flagship policy. We cover it in the second half of the chapter.

THERE AREN'T ENOUGH JOBS

The Great Depression, which started in 1929 in the United States, sent shock waves around the world. One of its most prominent features was a dramatic increase in unemployment. In the United States, unemployment reached a peak of 25% in 1933. In the United Kingdom, it reached a peak of 23% the same year. Unemployment dropped very slowly thereafter and remained high well into the 1940s.

British economist John Maynard Keynes was extremely unsettled by the eyewatering level of unemployment and tried to find an explanation for it. In 1936, he published an influential book called *The General Theory of Employment, Interest, and Money*. Keynes thought that the classical theory of unemployment—which said it was caused by rigid and overly high wages—was naive and couldn't explain the existence and persistence of the high levels of unemployment of that era. So, he took it upon himself to propose a novel theory.

Early in his book, Keynes promised his theory would have nothing to do with wage rigidity like the classical theory. He would prove that, even if wages were flexible and thus could be updated quickly, high unemployment would still exist and persist for a long time. He called this phenomenon *involuntary unemployment*. Let's take a tour of Keynes' theory.

Keynes thinks that unemployment is caused by entrepreneurs not creating a large-enough number of jobs. So, he starts his theory by explaining how entrepreneurs make hiring decisions. He says that they do so based on their expectations about their future sales and costs.

According to Keynes, entrepreneurs expect that hiring more people will help them collect more revenue. This is because employment generates welfare in the population, so the economy will do better, and consumers will spend more money.

Suppose you own a café, and you're wondering whether to hire a new barista. In your mind, you know that, by hiring a new barista, you're giving a new person the opportunity to work and thus to spend more. The economy does better as a result, which means you sell more coffee.

But there's a limit to this because increased hiring has diminishing returns. For example, if you keep hiring baristas, it will become harder with each new hire to coordinate their work effectively. So, at one point, the complications caused by hiring more baristas will outweigh the benefits, and your profits will take a hit.

Entrepreneurs settle for the sweet spot in between. They hire just the right number of people that they expect will generate good sales without eroding profits.[2]

According to Keynes, the resulting number of jobs could be anything. This is because the process relies on subjective predictions about uncertain future sales, which makes the process highly dependent on entrepreneurs' mood. Keynes calls this mood "animal spirits." If animal spirits run high, entrepreneurs are positive about the future and thus hire more people. If animal spirits run low, they're pessimistic and thus hire fewer people. Entrepreneurs may cling to their low expectations for a prolonged period, so they may create few jobs chronically.

It is likely that the number of jobs created will be less than "full employment," which Keynes roughly defines as an economy that is fully utilizing all of its available resources. For example, entrepreneurs may create fewer jobs than the total number of people who can work. According to Keynes, this explains the cause of unemployment and why it persists for a long time.

MMT says that Keynes' theory is the best explanation of unemployment that we have. So, it fully embraces it.

There are many problems with Keynes' theory. The first one is that it's hard to believe that it describes accurately how entrepreneurs make decisions. Would you think that by hiring an extra barista the economy will do better and thus your coffee sales will go up? Probably not. The same likely goes for large companies. Will Apple expect that by hiring more people it will sell more iPhones, as the general population will become wealthier and spend more? Probably not.

Back in 1959, journalist Henry Hazlitt complained:

> No manufacturer says to himself: "I shall hire N number of men, and this will give me total cash costs of Z and total cash receipts of D." He begins the other way round. He begins by deciding either how much money he can afford to lay out, say Z, or how much of a product he could make or sell, getting receipts of D. And then he decides how many men he will need or can afford ... Entrepreneurs practically never think or act in the way Keynes implies.[3]

MMT defends Keynes' position, arguing that the said behavior applies to the community of entrepreneurs as a whole and not to individual entrepreneurs. MMTer William Mitchell explains:

> Even if this might not be true for some firms, it will likely be true of all firms taken together.[4]

This isn't very convincing. If not a single entrepreneur in the group thinks this way, why would the entire group as a whole do?[5]

Mitchell adds:

> As employment rises, firms in the aggregate will expect greater revenue from sales.[6]

But this conflates two different time periods—the present and the future. What Keynes tries to explain is how firms make decisions in the present based on predictions about the future, not how these decisions may change in the future as the economy does better.

Confusingly, Mitchell adds that the theory proposed by Keynes

> is a tool that we as economists can use to think about the determination of employment at the aggregate level of the economy. Individual firms do not use the framework to determine their own level of employment.[7]

This is strange. Even if this theory were just a tool for economists, it's unclear why such tool would rely on unrealistic assumptions about entrepreneurs' behavior.

Another issue is that Keynes abandoned the study of unemployment, which should reveal why people can't find a job. Instead, he studied employment, which describes how many people have a job. These concepts are related but different. The fact that a certain number of people have a job doesn't tell us much about why so many other people are struggling to finding one. It also doesn't tell us how the unemployment rate may itself influence entrepreneurs' and workers' decisions. As a result, Keynes' theory is, at best, incomplete.

Also, note that Keynes defines "full employment" in a way that has little to do with unemployment. He thinks of full employment as an economy's maximum possible resource utilization. This mixes up different productive resources, such as workers and machines. It also ignores that some people may not want to work—they may choose to retire, study, be stay-at-home parents, and so on.[8] MMT echoes this confusion, sometimes using the term "full employment" to mean zero unemployment and other times to mean "maximum possible resource utilization."

But there's an even bigger and more dramatic problem with Keynes' theory.

If you remember, Keynes says that entrepreneurs perform calculations of future profitability in their minds. For this, they must estimate their costs. Otherwise, they wouldn't be able to determine profitability. One of the most important costs is the wage they pay their employees.

Keynes assumes that the wage is a fixed number, say, $15 an hour, and cannot be changed or negotiated. This is extremely surprising. If you remember, one of Keynes' main goals was to prove that a rigid wage had nothing to do with unemployment. So why assume that the wage is rigid? Economist Michel De Vroey calls this procedure "rather odd."[9]

Keynes justifies his decision on pedagogical grounds. He says that his assumption that the wage is rigid "is introduced solely to facilitate the exposition,"[10] but it doesn't change his conclusions in any way.

Unfortunately, Keynes' assumption proves fatal to his theory. Wage rigidity is the only reason we find, within his entire book, to explain why unemployment can persist for a long time. Perhaps the reason why "animal spirits" are persistently low is precisely *because* wages cannot be renegotiated—ever—so wages can remain at a prohibitively high level. No wonder entrepreneurs are so pessimistic in Keynes' world!

So, Keynes' theory is nothing new, as it places the blame for prolonged unemployment on rigid wages, just like the previous theories did—the ones Keynes wanted to debunk. Economist Axel Leijonhufvud explains:

> The rigid wage hypothesis was not a novel idea in Keynes' day. That the explanation of why labor fails to sell must start from the presumption that wages are too high and won't come down is a notion that is in all probability older than is economics as a discipline.[11]

In Chapter 19 of his book, after assuming the wage was rigid for hundreds of pages, Keynes tries to remove this fatal assumption. He tries to demonstrate that, even if the wage was allowed to change, his conclusion would remain intact—unemployment would remain high and persist over time regardless of the wage.

This was Keynes' last opportunity to salvage his theory. Let's take a quick tour of Chapter 19.

WAGES DON'T MATTER

Imagine you own a café and are on the fence about hiring a new barista. But, at some point, the typical barista wage goes down from, say, $15 an hour to $10 an hour. This could be, for example, due to a change in employment law. As a result, you decide to hire a new barista.

But what happens afterward? According to Keynes, you will face severe negative consequences due to the reduced wage. So, the decision to pay a lower wage will come back to bite you.

For example, people will have less money to spend—due to the reduced wage—so they will buy less coffee overall. This will hurt your sales.

In addition, the lower wage will make it cheaper to run cafés in general, so you will face tougher competition from other cafés. As a result, you will have to lower the price at which you sell your coffee, and this will further hurt your sales. It's an unfortunate "chain reaction."

Your sales will suffer so much that all the initial benefits of the lower wage will be *completely* wiped out. Due to your poor sales figures, you decide to fire the barista you've just hired. You're back to square one—your café has the same number of employees it started with.

So, Keynes concludes that the wage doesn't affect the number of jobs created by entrepreneurs. It can only cause a short-lived spike in employment. But Keynes explains that, ultimately, sales revenue "will disappoint the entrepreneurs and employment will fall back again to its previous figure."[12]

Keynes concludes:

> There is, therefore, no ground for the belief that a flexible wage policy is capable of maintaining a state of full employment.[13]

Keynes' theory has numerous problems. For starters, Keynes seems to believe that a drop in the wage rate, say, from $15 an hour to $10 an hour, makes the overall population poorer, and, as a result, they will spend less. But this isn't necessarily true if more people are employed as a result. For example, two baristas making $10 an hour make more money than one barista making $15 an hour and an unemployed barista making $0 an hour.

In addition, it is hard to believe that the negative consequences of a lower wage will *exactly* wipe out all the benefits it provides to entrepreneurs. For example, even if you have to lower your coffee price due to increased competition, it's unlikely this will offset your lower spending on wages dollar by dollar.

Moreover, Keynes' analyzes the effect of replacing a certain fixed wage with another, lower fixed wage. Keynes doesn't explain how the wage is determined, and it excludes the possibility of wage negotiation between workers and entrepreneurs.[14]

Despite all its glitches, MMTers defend Keynes' explanation. They say that, when the wage is in "the normal range," what Keynes says is true—changes in the wage have no effect on unemployment. However, they don't explain what the "normal range" is, how it's calculated, and why Keynes' mechanism works within that range.[15]

In the preface of his book, Keynes said that his readers

> will fluctuate, I expect, between a belief that I am quite wrong and a belief that I am saying nothing new.[16]

Well, he got that right.

Keynes didn't convince readers, and his theory fell into oblivion.[17] It is not even mentioned in most current economics textbooks.[18] But Keynes' theory never seems to die off completely. A small group of economists, which includes MMTers, still find it convincing and are ready to defend it with all their animal spirits.

A CHRONIC DISEASE

Due to their belief in Keynes' theory, MMTers think it is a proven fact that the private sector will always create a largely insufficient number of jobs. MMTer Stephanie Kelton says:

> The market price of an unemployed worker is zero—that is, no one is currently bidding on them.[19]

In addition, MMT describes unemployment as a chronic disease. This is because, following Keynes' explanation, there are no market forces, such as wage adjustments, that could help reduce unemployment. MMTer Éric Tymoigne explains:

> Unemployment is a permanent feature of capitalist economies ... There are chronically not enough jobs available for those willing to work regardless of how well-trained and motivated individuals are and how fair and easy it is to access the job market.[20]

MMT proposes a clear-cut solution to fix the problem: the government should give a job to anyone who wants one. The "MMT lens" helps us see that the government can always afford this, as it can create as much money as needed. In addition, the MMT lens helps us see that this policy won't have any negative consequences, such as inflation. This is because the policy just mobilizes idle resources—unemployed people that the private sector doesn't want to hire under any circumstances. By offering jobs to everyone, the problem of unemployment is completely solved.

Let's discuss this ambitious—and controversial—policy proposal.

THE JOB GUARANTEE PROGRAM

MMT proposes to solve unemployment through a program called *job guarantee*, or *JG*. This means that the government offers a job to anyone who wants one. MMTer Stephanie Kelton says, "MMT fights involuntary unemployment by eliminating it."[21]

JG jobs are paid by the central government, which may use its power to create money to pay for it.

A JG job must pay a good living wage. MMTer Éric Tymoigne explains:

> For MMTers, JG employment should pay a living wage with generous benefits (healthcare, paid sick leave, paid vacations, etc.).[22]

To make things easy, MMTers suggest setting the wage to the "current legal minimum wage."[23]

The JG program is different from ordinary unemployment benefits in that it provides a much more generous, living wage for an indefinite amount of time, and it also gives people actual work to do.

While the central government pays the bill, it does not directly offer work. Instead, it makes JG workers available to "local, municipal governments as well as nonprofits and/or social enterprises and cooperatives."[24] These organizations can hire people from the pool of available JG workers, paid for by the central government.

JG workers must be hired to work on projects that benefits local communities. Éric Tymoigne suggests that some of these jobs could be

> working as a school aid, picking up trash on remote areas of the coastline, restoring natural habitats, providing company to lonely elders, providing access to clean water, constructing shelters for the homeless, preparing and distributing food for the destitute, or removing invasive species, among many other activities.[25]

MMTer Randall Wray adds:

> Have we become so blind that we cannot see our failing infrastructure, our understaffed parks with their closed swimming pools and unkempt trails, the unmet needs of our seniors and our children, our polluted ponds and streams that require clean-up, and our low-income housing that would benefit from repairs and insulation? Are we really so unimaginative that we cannot think of a way to match our jobless with paid work tackling the unmet tasks surrounding us?[26]

(By the way, I must admit this made me giggle a little. I thought to myself, "First-world problems!")

According to MMT, the JG program acts like a buffer against the needs of the private sector. If the private sector goes through a bout of positive "animal spirits," it will want to hire many people. So, the pool of JG workers will shrink because the private sector will hire people away from the JG program. If, on the contrary, animal spirits run low, the private sector will want to employ fewer people. So, the size of the JG pool expands.

Voilà. Unemployment is virtually eliminated, forever. But this may be too good to be true. Let's see.

THE INFLATION CHALLENGE

Critics believe that the JG program would cause an inflation problem. By offering a guaranteed job that pays minimum wage, JG jobs would compete with the private sector for workers. The private sector would have to pay a premium to hire people out of the JG pool, as some workers may prefer JG jobs to private employment.

Imagine you lose your job and enter the JG pool. You now make the same money as before—or close to it—and have plenty of benefits. Perhaps you even have a pretty relaxed job providing company to the elderly. It is conceivable that you may want the private sector to offer you a higher salary to incentivize you to quit your JG job.

As private jobs must pay a premium to hire workers out of the JG pool, they are likely to pass on some of the increased costs to consumers. Many economists think this would cause "cost-push inflation," meaning that prices of products and services would increase all around the economy due the increased cost of labor.

But this initial increase in prices poses a problem to the JG program. As prices go up, the JG wage no longer provides the living standard it used to. JG workers feel they've lost purchasing power. If the government is true to its promise of providing a good living standard to JG workers, then it must increase the JG wage.

This causes a wage-price spiral. As the government increases the JG wage, it causes another wage increase in the private sector—to compete against JG jobs. This causes another increase in prices, as companies pass on their higher costs to consumers. The government must then increase the JG wage again as a result, thus triggering a new round of wage increases in the private sector, followed by price increases, and so on. The wage-price spiral never ends.

MMTers deny this. They argue that the program hires "off the bottom" by paying minimum wage, so it doesn't affect the private job market.[27] But this argument doesn't hold up. In most countries, the market for minimum-wage jobs is large. So, a sizable portion of the population would be affected by the program.

Some MMTers argue they've used sophisticated mathematical models to prove that the JG program wouldn't cause inflation. However, their models make strange assumptions. For example, they assume 0% of people working at minimum wage in the private sector would take a JG job.[28]

MMTers also argue that there can be no inflation because JG jobs simply mobilize idle resources not wanted by the private sector. MMTer William Mitchell explains:

> There can be no inflationary pressures arising directly from a policy where the government offers a fixed wage to any labour not wanted by other employers ... By definition, the unemployed have no market price because there is no market demand for their services.[29]

This argument arises from MMT's belief in Keynes' theory of unemployment, which says entrepreneurs just don't want to hire enough workers under any circumstances. As discussed before, this theory isn't very credible.

MMTers have sometimes accepted that the JG program could cause inflation. However, they say inflation would a "one-time" thing—prices will go up just once right after the program is set up.[30] This is hard to believe, as it ignores the rest of the spiral discussed earlier. MMTers ask us to believe that, after this initial "one-time" price hike, politicians will refuse to increase the JG wage to restore the living conditions offered previously by JG jobs.

MMT also argues that the JG program won't cause inflation because it expands the productive capacity of the economy, as JG workers gain new skills and contribute to public infrastructure. This makes it possible to produce more stuff, so there is less pressure for businesses to increase prices. MMTer Randall Wray says this effect would be so pronounced that it could even cause deflation—a generalized lowering of prices—as the capacity to produce stuff would be so significantly enhanced. The government may even need to cut down taxes to fight the threat of deflation.[31]

But it is hard to believe productive capacity would be enhanced by so much that the threat of inflation would disappear, let alone cause deflation. Could the skills gained on a JG job, say, by providing company to the elderly, enhance overall economic productivity in a significant way?

In addition, MMTers believe that the JG program would reduce hiring costs in the private sector, thus thwarting the threat of inflation. MMTer Éric Tymoigne explains:

> The JG should lower recruiting and hiring costs as employers would have an employed pool of workers demonstrating readiness and willingness to work, which should reduce inflation pressures ... A JG is a means for raising the employability of the unemployed by giving them an opportunity to learn or relearn work habits, gain some skills and training, and create a history of gainful employment.[32]

MMTer William Mitchell adds:

> The JG lowers the cost of hiring for firms because the JG workers do not experience the dislocation of unemployment and retain most, if not all, of their general and specific skills.[33]

But many people remain unconvinced. MMT critic Robert P. Murphy says:

> Why would employers be keen on hiring someone who has spent, say, the last three years working in the guaranteed job sector? This would be, by design, the cushiest job in America.[34]

We could also analyze the JG program from the point of view of the quantity of money created. According to MMT, the JG program would never end because "unemployment is the default state of affairs of capitalist economies."[35]

Suppose the never-ending program results in a permanently increased deficit, funded by the persistent creation of new money. As discussed in the previous chapter, this rings inflation bells to a lot of people, as there would be increasingly more money in the hands of the population.

MMTer Randall Wray doesn't agree. He says that the new money created to pay for the JG program would be hoarded instead of spent. He argues that the existence of unemployment proves "de facto" that the private sector is eager to save more money.[36] So, as money would be hoarded instead of spent, the JG program wouldn't cause inflation. This is a bit hard to believe.

Wray also says that the JG program may not even lead to increased government spending at all. He explains:

> It is possible that the program would "pay for itself" in terms of savings due to reduced crime, improved health, greater social and economic stability, and larger reductions in Medicaid.[37]

Once again, this is a bit hard to believe.

THE POLITICAL CHALLENGE

Critics believe the JG program would be riddled with political and implementation issues. One of the issues is that, if things work like MMTers say, the size of the pool of JG workers would be highly variable over time, as it would depend on the "animal spirits" of the private sector. So, the government wouldn't be able to count on JG workers to do any important work, as it would be an unreliable source of labor. Economics professor Malcom Sawyer explains that JG jobs "would have to be jobs which society (or at least the government) is rather indifferent ... as to whether they are undertaken."[38]

According to Sawyer, it wouldn't be acceptable to use "care of the elderly" as a source of JG jobs, as this would mean this type of care would be dependent on the fluctuations of the JG pool.[39]

In addition, Sawyer explains that government infrastructure projects "cannot be started, speeded up or delayed at short notice."[40] So, it's likely the government would have to hire workers the usual way—not from the JG pool—if it wants to provide a stable labor force for these projects.

As JG workers may not be able to do important stuff, they may end up doing unimportant or make-believe work. This has worried people all over the political spectrum, including those who support more government intervention in the economy. For example, MMT critic Thomas Palley says, "Such instances of make-work activity are then likely to be used by neoliberal politicians to attack government in general."[41]

Another political problem is that local governments, nonprofits, social enterprises, and so on have two different and conflicting ways of hiring people. One way is the usual way—they hire workers and pay their wages using their own budgets. The other one is the JG way—they hire "free" workers whose wages are paid for by the central government. Some people fear this could make them prefer the "free" workers over ordinary workers, and they would try to bargain down on the wage and benefits of existing workers hired in the traditional way. MMT critic Thomas Palley says that the JG program "could be used to undermine public sector wages and public sector unions."[42]

I also wonder who will determine which organizations are allowed to hire JG workers and which aren't and who will ensure that the work done by JG workers in these organizations benefits local communities. I wonder whether these decisions could cause further political tension and administrative overhead.

MMT doesn't provide satisfactory solutions to these issues. In most cases, it doesn't acknowledge them.[43] In other cases, it acknowledges that there could be issues, but it only provides general recommendations to address them. For example, MMTer Éric Tymoigne says, "To be less disruptive, the implementation of a JG can be ramped up over several years"[44] without explaining how it should be ramped up or what the schedule would be. He also says that problems could be reduced by "recognizing errors and improving design"[45] without providing convincing details.

Sometimes MMTers mention that JG-like programs have been successfully implemented in the past. They often cite a program called *Jefes*, which was launched in Argentina in 2002, as a stellar example of a successful JG-like program.[46]

I was surprised when I first saw this, as my own recollection of this program—which was run when I was a child in Argentina—is much less rosy than MMTers claim. For starters, the wage paid was extremely low and insufficient to cover basic nutritional needs.[47] I don't recall anyone thinking of this program as a way of having a guaranteed job that offered good living standards.

In addition, the program wasn't universal. Instead, it only offered a job to one person per household—the *jefe*, or "boss"—but only if one member of the household was underage, disabled, or pregnant.

As far as I recall, the program was surrounded by controversy due to its numerous implementation issues. It's been reported that 40–58% of participants were never given any work to do.[48]

The program ended in 2005, three years after it was launched, and it was replaced by a social transfer program in which qualifying households received a subsidy without being given work to do.[49]

FINAL THOUGHTS

Economists are human beings. So, even if they're driven by their best intentions, they can sometimes get a little too carried away by their political beliefs. I have the impression that Keynes was at least partly politically motivated when he developed his theory of unemployment. He seemed a little too eager to prove that unemployment was a chronic disease caused by entrepreneurs and that only the government could heal it.

Keynes made numerous mistakes—he contradicted himself repeatedly, used the same terms to mean different things, and made dubious assumptions, among other issues. Many economists think this was because Keynes wanted to formulate a theory that fit his prior political beliefs.[50]

My impression is that MMTers may also be politically motivated. They seem to believe, as a matter of principle, that unemployment is an inevitable chronic disease of market economies. So, they've picked the unemployment theory that best fits this belief—Keynes' long-disproven theory. They seem so eager to defend their beliefs that they're willing to reproduce and amplify the glitches in Keynes' theory.

MMTers seem to also have decided, as a matter of principle, that the job guarantee program is the best way to solve unemployment. So, they're willing to overlook any problems with the proposed program and defend it using dubious and contradictory arguments.

The lack of a sound unemployment theory and the lack of a sound solution make MMT's proposals not very workable.

But there's one arena in which MMTers have certainly succeeded. Just like Keynes back in the day, they've managed to widely promote their suspicious ideas to the general public and captivate the public's imagination.

In the next and final chapter of this book, we discuss other policies proposed by MMT, which are intended to protect the planet, foster prosperity, and more.

CHAPTER SIX

HOW TO SAVE THE PLANET AND INCREASE PROSPERITY

The proponents of MMT are deeply concerned about the greatest societal challenges of our era, and they think we shouldn't let our money worries get in the way of solving them. MMTer Yeva Nersisyan says:

> Can we afford the costs of avoiding annihilation? ... The costs of extinction of the human species—from the point of view of humans, at least—is beyond measure. Even if we calculate the costs of the Green New Deal as $93 trillion (as one hysterical estimate puts it) over the next decade, that is puny in comparison with the discounted cost of total destruction of human life on planet Earth.[1]

In the last chapter, we discussed MMT's solution to unemployment. In this chapter, we'll go further and discuss other policies proposed by MMT to tackle wider challenges.

We start with the Green New Deal, a proposed environmental and social reform in the United States. The point of this section is not specifically to discuss the merits of the Green New Deal. Instead, the point is to show how MMT proposes analyzing a policy. We will learn, through a practical example, how MMT replaces the pervasive "household" analysis.

After discussing the Green New Deal, we'll comment on other policy aspects of MMT, including monetary sovereignty and interest rates. We'll finish with a look into the future, by discussing how MMT recommends fostering economic growth.

Let's get started!

THE GREEN NEW DEAL

The Green New Deal is a major environmental reform, which has been proposed in different versions around the world. We'll focus on the US version, which is the most famous one, and it's the one MMTers have analyzed.

The Green New Deal proposes tackling climate change through major investments to replace fossil-based electricity production with renewables. In addition, it proposes numerous infrastructure improvements to reduce energy consumption, such as the insulation of houses.

But the Green New Deal isn't just "green." It also includes numerous social reforms, such as a job guarantee program inspired by MMT. In addition, it proposes a complete overhaul of the US healthcare system, replacing it with a single-payer, government-funded system like the one in the United Kingdom. It also proposes the immediate relief of all student debt and free college education for all.

In 2019, a Green New Deal resolution was brought in front of the US Senate.² While the bill didn't pass, the attempt made headlines, and the Green New Deal gained widespread attention.

MMT can be used to analyze the Green New Deal in a novel way. MMTer Yeva Nersisyan wrote a detailed report that performs such an analysis.³ This is one of the most concrete and practical examples of how MMT can be used for policymaking. It also shows us how government finances could be run differently once we abandon the "household" way of thinking.

Let's go through Nersisyan's report.

It starts by reminding us that we shouldn't think about "affordability," as the government can afford anything it wants thanks to its capacity to create money. Instead, we should analyze the Green New Deal in terms of the actual productive resources required to carry it out, such as machines, workers, and materials. Nersisyan explains:

> We need to obtain an inventory of the resources that can be made available to the Green New Deal projects to compare with the resources that will be required to implement the Green New Deal. This would include resources in excess supply plus those that can be released from uses that will be eliminated by the adoption of the Green New Deal. This is the true "cost" of the Green New Deal.⁴

When I first read this, I found it pretty promising. Keeping a tally of actual resource requirements, say, solar panels, is a welcome contribution to the environmental discussion. It seems pertinent to discuss whether we have the capacity to produce the required solar panels, insulate homes, and so on. If not, how can we increase that capacity?

But not so fast! There is an unexpected twist to this story.

Immediately after, Nersisyan admits that keeping a tally of resource requirements and availability is difficult. So, she suggests taking a shortcut. Instead of keeping track of a complicated inventory of resources, she will use spending—in money terms—as a proxy for resources. For example, if a component of the Green New Deal is expected to cost one billion dollars, we can think of it as one billion dollars' worth of "resources."

Let's go through Nersisyan's calculations.

We start with the transition to renewable energy. Nersisyan estimates that this will cost $1.03 trillion a year for 10 years, based on the calculations performed by other researchers. Following the proposed shortcut, we interpret this as $1.03 trillion worth of "resources" required to implement this ambitious plan.

The next item is the job guarantee program. Nersisyan calculates that the government will spend $400 billion a year to pay the wages of job guarantee workers.

But this isn't the end of the story. Many of these workers will be put to work on Green New Deal tasks, such as installing solar panels. So, Nersisyan estimates that half of the wage bill will "pay for itself" by supplying useful greening work.[5] As a result, we can ignore half of the wage bill and consider that the job guarantee only requires $200 billion worth of "resources."

Let's move on to the miscellaneous components of the Green New Deal, such as wiping out student debt, free college, and general infrastructure improvements.

Nersisyan argues that all these components increase workers' productivity. For example, free college trains people, which makes them more effective at work. So, whatever resources are required to offer free college are *completely* offset by the new resources supplied by the more productive workforce. As a result, free college "pays for itself."[6] So, we don't need to count it when analyzing the Green New Deal. No calculations are offered by Nersisyan to justify this. The same logic is then applied to the other miscellaneous components of the Green New Deal, which are also assumed to pay for themselves.

So far, we're up a total of $1.23 trillion new "resources" required to implement the Green New Deal, which come from only two components: the energy transition and the job guarantee program.

Where will all these resources come from? Let's see.

According to Nersisyan, the healthcare reform will dramatically *reduce* how much money Americans spend every year on healthcare. She estimates that a UK-style healthcare system will reduce such spending by $760 billion.[7] By using the MMT shortcut, this is interpreted as $760 billion worth of freed up "resources" that can be used to carry out other projects. For example, they can be used to carry out the energy transition component of the Green New Deal.

In addition, Nersisyan analyzes a Green New Deal item called "end the forever wars." This initiative reduces military spending by $200 billion. This is interpreted as $200 billion worth of "resources" that are freed up for other uses, such as energy transition.

So, there's a total of $860 billion freed-up "resources," which are supplied by the reduction in healthcare and military spending.

To conclude, Nersisyan compares the resources required by the first few components of the Green New Deal with the resources freed up by the latter components:

	Resources Required (+) or Freed Up (−)
Greening projects	+ $1.03 T
Job guarantee	+ $200 B
Miscellaneous	+ $0
Healthcare reform	− $760 B
End forever wars	− $200 B
All together	+ $270 B

The result is that the Green New Deal almost pays for itself, as the $1.23 trillion "resources" required by the first few components are offset by the $860 billion "resources" freed-up by the other components.

The difference between the two is only $270 billion. We interpret this as follows: The Green New Deal only requires mobilizing $270 billion worth of additional "resources" every year than are currently mobilized. To put things in perspective, Nersisyan compares this figure with GDP, which is an estimate of the total yearly economic production; $270 billion corresponds to "only" 1.3% of GDP. It turns out that saving the planet wasn't that hard after all!

If you remember, MMT says that inflation takes place when we try to use more resources than are available. Nersisyan concludes it's very unlikely the Green New Deal will cause inflation. This is because there's probably enough slack in the economy, in the form of unused resources lying around, to increase production by a meagre 1.3%.

But what if people still feared this reform could cause inflation? Nersisyan proposes to "allay fears of inflation" by introducing a temporary tax on workers' wages. She clarifies this is not to "raise revenue" but to make people "defer consumption" a little bit and thus provide additional resources for the Green New Deal. If this doesn't work, Nersisyan proposes introducing "price controls, rationing, and additional taxes."[8]

Unfortunately, this analysis doesn't hold up very well. For starters, it doesn't analyze real productive resources, contrary to MMT's big promise. Instead, MMT uses spending—in terms of money—in a rough and aggregated way to represent "resources." This isn't particularly insightful or novel.

In addition, MMT assumes all resources are alike and can be easily repurposed. For example, the healthcare reform frees up resources that can be used for energy transition. But will a former health insurance broker be able to install solar panels? Will a pharmaceutical salesperson be able to operate a power plant?

Similarly, MMT assumes that reduced military spending will free up resources for energy transition. But can a machine designed to produce bullets be repurposed to produce solar panels? Can a soldier operate a power plant?

Another issue with MMT's approach is that its calculations are extremely suspicious. Too many things just "pay for themselves" by assumption. This is hard to believe. Will free college increase productivity by so much that we can assume it to be costless?

Moreover, in this analysis, the healthcare reform provides the vast majority of the "resources" used for energy transition. But I doubt its calculations are realistic. It is true that Americans pay remarkably high prices for healthcare compared to, say, UK residents. However, they also access a higher volume of care, including more diagnostic tests and elective surgeries.[9] So, Americans would have to change their habits to reduce their healthcare spending by as much as predicted by MMT.

All in all, MMT's analysis does not provide a credible example of how MMT can be used for serious policymaking. And it provides no useful insights about how we can protect the planet.

MONETARY SOVEREIGNTY

During the 1980s, El Salvador experienced high inflation, which surpassed 30% a year. This wasn't as dramatic as in neighboring Latin American countries, which suffered from hyperinflation, but it was high enough to unsettle Salvadoreans. In the 1990s, inflation dropped significantly. Former Minister of Finance Manuel Hinds explains:

> We passed a law forbidding the central bank from financing the government, period ... Inflation went down because the government was not printing money ... The government substantially reduced its fiscal deficit because it could no longer go to the central bank and tell the central bank to give me money.[10]

But something rather strange happened afterward. Despite the low inflation rate, commercial banks were still charging eye-watering interest rates on loans. Manuel Hinds explains:

> When I became the Minister of Finance, inflation was already very low, and the next year, the inflation was 2% ... But then, the problem we had was that the rate of interest was very high. If you wanted to borrow money for a house, you would get an interest rate of 24%.[11]

Something didn't seem quite right. According to Hinds, the reason for this phenomenon was that people

> didn't believe that the government would no longer devalue the currency or print money. They said, these guys who are in the government right now, are not going to print money, and they are not going to devalue the currency, but what about the next one?[12]

So, it wasn't enough to stop creating money. People had to believe *future* governments would not start creating money all over again. According to Hinds, the public simply didn't buy it.

Hinds and his team engineered a plan to solve this issue: abandon El Salvador's national currency. They proposed adopting the US dollar instead, which would become El Salvador's official currency. As a result, future governments wouldn't be able to create money (unless they reintroduced a national currency, which would be quite a hassle).

The proposal was initially met with widespread opposition, especially due to the loss of sovereignty that it signified. Hinds failed to get his plan approved. During a 2024 interview, in which he looked back into that era, Hinds explained:

> They were saying we are going to lose sovereignty and we had this other argument saying, "You're calling sovereignty the ability for the Minister of Finance to have some drinks and then, devalue the currency."
>
> Do you think that you are sovereign? People prefer the dollar because at the time already if you wanted to have a contract, this happens in Argentina, if you want to sign a contract to lease an apartment, then you have to do it in dollars. Everything was in dollars, but people say, no, no, no, our sovereignty.[13]

In 2000, however, a subsequent government analyzed Hinds' proposal more thoroughly and approved it, as it determined it could improve stability and promote trade with other countries. On January 1, 2001, the US dollar become El Salvador's official currency, and the national currency was abandoned. The country has been using US dollars since then, although there was a failed attempt to introduce Bitcoin as an alternative currency in 2021.[14]

El Salvador isn't the only country in Latin America to abandon its national currency. In 2000, Ecuador did the same. The Ecuadorian story is bitterer though. Ecuador was experiencing economic turmoil and high inflation at the time, and the fear of hyperinflation was simmering. During this crisis, the country adopted the US dollar as an emergency measure to tame inflation and placate the fear of hyperinflation. The US dollar has been Ecuador's currency since then.[15]

In 2023, during Argentina's latest surge of inflation, presidential candidate Javier Milei promised to abandon the national currency too.[16] At first, I must admit I didn't quite understand his proposal. Milei thought inflation was caused by the government creating money to pay its bills. So, why not just stop that practice? Why go as far as eliminating the national currency? I understood the rationale after speaking with a local economist. He told me that, much like in El Salvador, the point was to prevent future governments—whether Milei was in power or not—from resorting to money creation to fund their spending. As of this writing, Argentina still uses its national currency, as Milei has found his proposed reform technically and politically difficult to pull off.

The threat of inflation is not the only reason why countries abandon their national currencies. In 1999, eleven European countries did so for other reasons. They adopted a new, common currency called the euro, managed by a supranational entity called the European Central Bank. Their goal was to promote trade and economic integration among member countries.[17] Nine more European countries joined the eurozone over the next few years.

So, different monetary arrangements are possible. At one end of the spectrum, the country has a *sovereign currency*, which means it creates its own currency and doesn't promise to exchange it against anything else.

At the other end, a country exclusively adopts a foreign currency, such as the US dollar in Ecuador.

MMT argues that currency sovereignty offers the most *policy space* to the government. This is the arrangement that gives the government the most wiggle room. For example, it can run a job guarantee program or implement the Green New Deal without worrying about affordability or debt. MMTer Randall Wray writes:

> The government has much more leeway (called "domestic policy space") when it spends and taxes in its own currency than when it spends or taxes in a foreign currency ... Sovereign currency → most policy space; government can "afford" anything for sale in its own currency. No default risk in its own currency. Inflation and currency depreciation are possible outcomes if government spends too much.[18]

Abandoning the national currency is frowned upon by MMTers. Randall Wray explains:

> The separation of a nation from its currency puts unnecessary constraint on fiscal policy that will almost certainly lead to a crisis.[19]

MMTers particularly dislike the eurozone arrangement. This is because the manager of the currency—the European Central Bank—does not conduct *fiscal policy* in member countries, which means using taxes and government spending to influence economies. For example, the European Central Bank does not collect income taxes or run a job guarantee program. So, the "leeway" offered by monetary sovereignty is not exploited. MMTer William Mitchell explains:

> What is highly questionable is the way in which monetary integration was pursued: with minimal concern for fiscal integration, so that individual European nations lost their currency sovereignty while no federal sovereign fiscal institution was created ... In this framework, individual national states are constrained because they cannot freely use fiscal instruments to affect output and employment.[20]

MMT acknowledges that currency sovereignty can have downsides too. They say its main downside is the instability caused by fluctuations of the exchange rate against foreign currencies. But you needn't worry! William Mitchell proposes a solution:

> Adopt a job guarantee that automatically ensures full employment while also helping to stabilize wages and prices.[21]

I'll add three caveats to MMT's analysis. First, using a non-sovereign currency, such as the euro in France, may facilitate trade and economic integration among different countries. This was one of the motives for the creation of the euro. Trade benefits must be factored in when we analyze the pros and cons of currency sovereignty. This isn't to say that losing currency sovereignty is necessarily a good idea. Not being able to control your currency isn't a decision to be taken lightly, as it puts you at the mercy of somebody else's decisions and policies, but it must be analyzed holistically.

Second, I'm not sure you gain so much "leeway" from having a sovereign currency. It is true that the government can do more things with it. For example, with suitable arrangements, it can create money to wipe out its debt or hand out stimulus checks to the population during a crisis. It can also implement a job guarantee program and wipe out student debt without worrying about "finding the money" to pay for it.

But these policies may not provide genuine economic gains. For example, suppose handing out stimulus checks causes a bout of inflation. As a result, anybody who has cash savings loses purchasing power, as their savings can buy them less stuff than before. It's as if savers were paying for the stimulus checks themselves through the erosion of the value of their money. Some economists call this an "inflation tax." So, the alleged MMT leeway may not generate true economic gains. However, paying for a program using an "inflation tax" may be easier to pull off politically compared to, say, an unpopular income tax.

In addition, MMTers have struggled to provide concrete examples of how the alleged leeway can be used in a productive way to do good. Their proposals—the job guarantee program, the Green New Deal, and so on— are not convincing.

Finally, what if monetary sovereignty is used irresponsibly? It could be like releasing a bull in a china shop.

There is widespread fear that money creation could be used irresponsibly by politicians. It was one of the reasons for the adoption of US dollars in El Salvador, and it's driving the same discussion in Argentina. Also, note that much of the popularity of cryptocurrencies is precisely because it eliminates the government's freedom to create money. Crypto supporters don't think governments use this power judiciously, so they think it should be removed. (I'm not sure crypto solves the problem though, as it's very easy to launch new cryptocurrencies out of the blue.)

Some people are even afraid monetary sovereignty could be used by the government to implement unpopular policies, which wouldn't be accepted if taxes had to be raised to pay for them. Bitcoin proponent Saifedean Ammous thinks that World War I was prolonged by the fact that governments used money creation to pay for it. He argues that, if the government had used ordinary taxes instead,

> It is likely that World War I would have been settled militarily within a few months of conflict, as one of the allied factions started running out of financing and faced difficulties in extracting wealth from a population that was not willing to part with its wealth to defend their regime's survival.[22]

What would happen if MMTers were put in charge of running government finances with a sovereign currency? Would they be able to find and exploit their "leeway" in a productive way, and thus generate genuine economic gains for the population? Or will it be like releasing a bull in a china shop?

ZERO INTEREST RATE

When inflation surged in 2021, central banks around the world increased *the interest rate*. The words "interest rate" made their way to the news much more often than usual.

Central banks monitor very closely the interest rate that commercial banks, such as HSBC, charge for lending money to one another. The central bank sets a target on this rate, and it intervenes the lending market to actively influence it so it's always close to the central bank's target. When people say "the" interest rate, this is the rate they're usually talking about.

Changes in the interest rate affect other interest rates around the economy. For example, if the interest rate goes up, the interest rates on mortgages and business loans go up too. This is because, if banks find it more expensive to borrow from one another, they also charge more for lending to their clients.

Central banks manipulate the interest rate to keep inflation under control. When inflation becomes high, the central bank increases the interest rate. The central bank hopes this will make the economy slow down because people will borrow less money to buy houses, businesses will borrow less to run new projects, and so on. This slowdown is expected to dampen inflation.

MMT is against using the interest rate to fight inflation. It argues that it is an ineffective policy, as businesses and individuals are not really that sensitive to interest rates. MMTer Éric Tymoigne explains:

> While some areas, such as housing, are more sensitive to changes in interest rates, overall interest rates do not play a major role in determining spending, especially business investment.[23]

In addition, MMT argues that an increase in the interest rate can cause instability and a surge of prices, as businesses may pass their higher financing costs to consumers. Moreover, richer people will collect higher interests from lending their money, which could make them consume more and thus increase inflation.[24]

As a result, MMT suggests setting the interest rate to zero. This is known as zero interest-rate policy, or ZIRP (rhymes with burp). ZIRP was implemented extensively after the 2008 financial crisis, together with quantitative easing, to stimulate economic activity. It ended in 2021, after the global surge of inflation.

MMT says that the interest rate should be parked at zero indefinitely. So, ZIRP should be the default policy. As a result, the general public would access cheap loans indefinitely. If inflation is ever to be fought, this should be done the MMT way—by increasing taxes and perhaps implementing price controls.

Economists aren't quite convinced that this is a good idea for multiple reasons. For starters, they think it could cause reckless loan-taking and investing. MMT critic Thomas Palley says that it "becomes a recipe for encouraging financial speculation and asset price inflation driven by debt, which ends in financial crisis."[25]

My intuition tells me there might be some truth to this argument. In the late 2010s and early 2020s, during the ZIRP era, there was a dramatic investment boom in tech start-ups. Some investments didn't seem to make much sense. For example, a company called Quibi received $1.8 billion from investors in one go to build a new video-streaming platform. The company didn't do a small test run to see if people were interested in the service. Instead, it went all-in and spent $1 billion in one go just to make fancy videos for the platform. The company collapsed six months after being launched. Other companies, such as WeWork, also received dramatic flows of investment—despite dubious business models—only to collapse later.

During this era, I spoke with many investors to understand what was going on, and many brought up the topic of low interest rates. They told me that this policy was responsible for the dramatic flow of funds into tech start-ups.[26] This was because money was cheap to obtain, and it was also difficult to get a good return from lending money to others. This encouraged risk-taking.

Another criticism of permanent ZIRP is that it eliminates the interest rate as a policy tool to fight inflation.[27] Some economists have been questioning the effectiveness of changes in the interest rate to fight inflation.[28] However, parking it at zero indefinitely would remove one tool from the toolbox. If inflation rises, we'd have to trust politicians to raise taxes to fight it. But politicians aren't big fans of doing that.

GROWTH

Economic growth has fascinated economists for decades. Economist Robert Lucas famously said, "Once you start thinking about growth, it's hard to think about anything else."

Economic growth is the increase in productive capacity of an economy—more stuff can be produced with less effort. This is the result of the accumulation of physical capital, such as machines and infrastructure, as well as technological innovation and the improvement of workers' skills. All these things make production easier.

As an economy grows, its population gets better bang for its effort. For example, an average worker may be able to buy a new fridge with a week's worth of wages instead of, say, a month or even months' worth of wages. For this reason, it is in general assumed that economic growth increases living standards, putting aside environmental sustainability and other caveats.

But economies don't always grow at the same rate over time, and some economies lag much further behind others.

Traditional economists think that subpar economic growth occurs due to a lack of investment in productivity enhancement tasks, such as building machines and infrastructure, training workers, and developing new technologies. So, to promote growth, the government should foster productivity-enhancing activities. For example, it may invest in infrastructure, such as a new port or highway. It should also develop political institutions that incentivize entrepreneurship, such as the enforcement of property rights.[29]

MMTers don't quite agree that this is the correct diagnosis and solution to the problem. They think that subpar growth is caused by perversive "slack" around the economy. If you remember, MMTers believe that entrepreneurs are pessimistic and chronically decide to hire too few people, run their factories well below capacity, and so on (see Chapter 5 on unemployment).

This generalized idleness harms long-term economic growth in numerous ways. First, unemployed workers lose their skills, which degrades productive capacity over time.[30] Second, companies are discouraged to enhance their own productivity because there are too many available idle resources they can use if needed. MMTer William Mitchell explains:

> Firms have little incentive to invest in training if unemployed workers are plentiful. Firms may simply raise their hiring standards to take advantage of slack labour markets. The inducement to invest is weak when existing capacity is underutilised. This leads to a slower rate of technological advance.[31]

MMTers often say that growth is "demand led," which means that it is driven by the total amount of spending in the economy—the more spending there is, the lower the slack, and the more businesses are incentivized to expand their operations, train workers, and so on.

So, MMT says that the best way to foster growth is to increase government spending. This causes a higher utilization of available resources, which promotes growth.[32] In other words, the government should "spend its way into prosperity."

But what if higher government spending causes inflation? MMTer Éric Tymoigne says we shouldn't worry about it. This is because increased government spending will promote growth, so the economy will soon expand to produce more stuff and absorb the additional spending. Tymoigne explains:

> Instead of tightening fiscal and monetary policy immediately as inflation rises (or even in anticipation of higher inflation), policymakers should give productive capacities time to adapt to the demand growth … While inflation may rise, it would be temporary.[33]

MMT's analysis isn't quite satisfactory. For starters, some of it seems illogical. For example, William Mitchell says that unemployment makes businesses reluctant to invest in training, as there are plenty of unemployed people available for hire. But where do all these unemployed people get their training from?

Second, MMT places too much emphasis on the role of idleness in low economic growth, while it underplays other factors. There is probably some truth to MMT's diagnosis. For example, unemployed people do miss out on gaining valuable skills, so their productivity is likely to decrease over time.[34] However, this is often seen as an aggravating factor and not the unique cause of slow economic growth.

Third, MMT's proposed solution seems a bit naive. Not all government spending is alike and equally conducive to growth. Some spending may be more directly conducive to growth, such as building a new port to facilitate trade. But, say, a job guarantee program may not be as conducive to growth. Suppose a job guarantee worker is given the task of providing company to the elderly. Would this enhance the productive capacity of the economy? Probably not by much.[35]

Finally, MMT assumes that productive capacity will be increased quickly enough to absorb increased government spending. In fact, you should let inflation rise, as the increase in capacity will dampen inflation.

This contradicts other MMT policy recommendations, which say taxes should be used to control inflation. It's also a dangerous leap of faith. How long can you ignore inflation for? And how can you be sure capacity will grow fast enough to dampen it? This hasn't worked in, say, Argentina, has it?

FINAL THOUGHTS

MMT says that, in countries that have monetary sovereignty, the government can make policy in a different way in order to exploit low-hanging opportunities and do good for its citizens. By following MMT's recipe, the government could tackle important societal issues, such as eliminating unemployment and protecting the planet.

Unfortunately, MMT hasn't provided convincing examples of how to do this. Its calculations are sloppy, and its policy recommendations are naive.

Moreover, all of MMT's policies seem to promote bigger and more encompassing government. This makes one wonder if MMT may be motivated by politics rather than by the wish to advance economic theory.

So, is MMT the key to prosperity or a recipe for disaster? The more I read about it, the more I get the impression that it's the latter.

CONCLUDING REMARKS: MMT AND THE FUTURE OF ECONOMICS

Thank you for getting this far. I hope you have found MMT as fascinating as I have. I will now draw some conclusions about MMT, and then I'll add some general comments about the field of economics, its convoluted history, and its future.

Let's start by briefly revisiting MMT's three principles, as described in the introduction, and see how the theory fairs against each of them.

THE THREE PRINCIPLES REVISITED

Principle 1: The Government Could Stop Worrying About Money

What MMT says is true—it is technically possible to let the government create money to pay its bills. The thing is, everybody knew this already! The question is not whether it's technically possible to do that. The question is whether it's a good idea. Most people think it's not a good idea for political reasons. Would you give politicians the power to create as much money as they want and trust they'll use it wisely? In addition, many people think it wouldn't make a big economic difference anyway, as the apparent gains from creating money could be offset by an "inflation tax."

Principle 2: The Government Already Creates New Money Daily to Pay for Stuff

MMT's analysis is incorrect. Most modern, real-life governments don't create money routinely to pay their bills. MMT reaches this incorrect conclusion due to an accounting error.

However, if central bank independence is eroded, the government may find it easier to create money to fund its spending. This could happen, for example, if quantitative easing is used in an unofficial way to help the government spend more or bail it out unconditionally. This could make the government more MMT-like in practice. Let's keep an eye out!

Principle 3: If We Loosen Restrictions on Government Spending, We Can Increase Prosperity

MMT fails to propose credible policies to eliminate unemployment, protect the planet, and increase welfare. Its proposed policies are based on naive economics and suffer from numerous practical issues. The free lunch we were promised is nowhere to be found.

Overall, MMT fails to fulfill its promises. We're left with a bitter impression that it's "policy leading to theory." MMT starts well—it makes interesting observations about the world and offers a legitimate alternative lens to understand the economy. But then it derails in its pursuit to justify its preferred policies. Its theorists seem willing to take dubious shortcuts and even contradict themselves to align the theory to their political goals.

Although MMT doesn't quite fulfill its promises, I think there are things we can learn from it. Let's have a look.

WHAT WE CAN LEARN FROM MMT

In my opinion, one of the virtues of MMT is that it helps us think more critically about the nature of fiat currency, which means currency issued by the government that cannot be exchanged against gold or anything else.

People often make fatalistic predictions about fiat currency. For example, I recently saw a social media post that said, "Fiat currency will be dead by 2037. The gold market is sending a clear signal. It has finally concluded that fiat is fake."

MMT helps us see that this is probably overly dramatic. MMT tells us that, at least to some extent, the obligation to pay taxes anchors the value of the national currency. For example, millions of US citizens and businesses must get ahold of US dollars to pay taxes every year, so it's unlikely the US dollar will completely collapse.

MMT has made me think more critically about Bitcoin. Many people are upset that fiat currency cannot be used for saving in the long run, due to inflation, and they argue that Bitcoin is a good alternative. But Bitcoin cannot be used to pay taxes, so what drives its value? MMT contributes to the conversation by showing that an important source of value for fiat currency—the obligation to pay taxes—is not present in Bitcoin. So, whatever Bitcoin's value is, it must come from somewhere else. I don't think I have yet found convincing arguments about where that value comes from and why it will persist (this is further discussed in Appendix A, if you're interested).

I think another virtue of MMT is that it has encouraged the general public to think about the "real" economy, meaning actual resources like materials, workers, and so on. It doesn't take money to build a hospital. What it "really" takes is physical resources. Money is the way in which we claim the right to utilize real resources. I think it's a good idea to always keep in mind that, behind the "money" economy, there's a "real" one.

In addition, MMT encourages us to distinguish "real" limits on government endeavors—such as the availability of materials to build a hospital—from "money" limits—such as the amount of money in the government's bank account and the debt ceiling imposed by Congress. The latter limits stem from our institutional arrangements and are imposed for political and economic reasons. But other arrangements are possible, including letting Nicolas Cage create as much money as he wants to buy Rolls Royces or letting an autocrat expropriate factories without pay. It's good to keep in mind the role of institutional arrangements whenever we hear things like "the government is running out of money" or "government debt is unsustainable."

THE FUTURE OF ECONOMICS

I recently had a chat with one of my high school teachers. She told me, "The world needs new economic theories." She's not alone—many people have grown increasingly concerned that economists haven't done a good job at explaining how economies work and proposing useful policies to tackle pressing issues.

Let's take a quick tour of the history of macroeconomics. We'll see that it's a bit convoluted and perhaps even a little embarrassing. We'll then discuss its future.

Macroeconomics started in the 1930s as a new, distinct branch of economics in response to the Great Depression. As opposed to microeconomics, which studies the behavior of individuals and firms, macroeconomics studies economy-wide phenomena, such as unemployment and inflation. Macroeconomics is thus especially interesting to inform policymaking that can affect the entire economy.

Macroeconomics went through two dramatically distinct phases.[1]

The first phase spanned 40 years, from the 1930s to the 1970s. During this time, economists focused most of their efforts on trying to explain unemployment and the nature of deep economic depressions. During this phase, researchers used very primitive methodologies, which were very practical but suffered from numerous problems.

For starters, economists defined terms in ambiguous and erratic ways, even important terms such as "involuntary unemployment." This made the literature confusing and sometimes contradictory. In addition, they often divided their theories into the "short term" and the "long term" without defining the boundary between the two. While this division was intuitively appealing, it made their theories internally inconsistent and ambiguous.

Moreover, economists rarely tried to understand how their economic laws arose from the decisions of people. Instead, they established general laws based on past observations without digging deeper.

To top it off, economists assumed the public wouldn't change its behavior if a new policy was announced. This meant people could be easily "tricked" to behave in ways that were beneficial to the policymaker.

This era covers the work of John Maynard Keynes and the people who followed his steps. It also covers the work of Keynes' main detractors of the time, such as Milton Friedman, who disagreed with Keynes but relied on similar methods to argue his case.

While economic understanding was improved in many ways during this period, the methodologies used left a lot to be desired. In retrospect, people have described them as "rules of thumb," "a conceptual mess," "policy without theory," and even "pre-scientific."[2]

I can't help but think how different this was from other disciplines, such as physics, which used much stronger methodologies during the same period and even earlier. Consider the special theory of relativity, which was presented by Einstein in 1905. Einstein started his presentation by describing two assumptions very precisely. He then deduced the entire theory just from those two assumptions, by following an unambiguous series of logical steps. Einstein presented an extended version of this theory in 1915, called the general theory of relativity. This theory was deduced just by adding one more assumption to the previous two and then following logical steps. Other researchers then continued the logical steps and got all the way to black holes and worm holes.

The methodological tidiness found in physics did not make its way to macroeconomics, despite both evolving at roughly the same time.

This changed dramatically in the 1970s, when a methodological revolution took place. This revolution was initiated by economist Robert Lucas, who challenged numerous aspects of the prevailing methods.

To make a long story short, this second generation of economics became a lot like physics.

In this new era, economists made clearly defined assumptions about the functioning of markets and the preferences of people and firms. They described these assumptions precisely and in mathematical terms, and they created a theoretical model of the economy. Afterward, they used fancy mathematical methods to deduce possible economic outcomes from interactions of people and firms in markets. The method became very similar to how physicists analyzed interactions between particles.

In this new era, economics became theoretically sounder, and economists started using common methods to approach different problems. It became much more beautiful than before.

But this new era of economics didn't turn out quite as expected.

In their quest to make economic theory mathematically beautiful, economists made unrealistic assumptions about people, firms, and markets. This made their theoretical models simple to work with, as equations were clean and easy to solve, but not very applicable to real life.

For example, economists often assumed there was one single household in the entire economy. This household was meant to represent the preferences of all households combined. In addition, their models contained no financial sector because banks were assumed to be just irrelevant intermediaries. Moreover, economists assumed unemployment was zero. If the number of people employed dropped, they assumed this was due to workers' increased preference for leisure.

The approach received much criticism after the 2008 financial crisis, as it failed to predict and explain the crisis. In fact, as the financial sector was assumed nonexistent in prevailing models, it was pretty much impossible to use them to analyze the crisis. In the aftermath of the crisis, economist Paul Krugman said, "Economists, as a group, mistook beauty, clad in impressive-looking mathematics, for truth."[3]

Since then, people have grown increasingly skeptical that mainstream economics can inform real-world policymaking, as it may be too far detached from reality. Economic historian Michel De Vroey says:

> Notwithstanding the progress that took place in macroeconomics, civil society should not have too high expectations about what present-day macroeconomic theory can deliver as far as policymaking is concerned. Likewise, macroeconomists should avoid pretending that they have an edge on policy matters and endorsing the role of expert that they are often unduly invited to play …[4]

Policy advisor Jeremy B. Rudd says:

> I came to a surprising realization: Very little of the theoretical or empirical research that has been done by mainstream academic macroeconomists was actually all that useful to me in my job as a policy economist ... A gap between academic and applied work that is this wide is disturbing ... It's difficult to understand why academic economists would be satisfied generating research that is of such little use to the people producing inputs to policy, or to anyone else who would like to understand how the economy actually works.[5]

So, what happens next? Since the financial crisis, economists have been working on extending their models to more complex and hopefully realistic scenarios. They're finally considering, for example, that the economy contains numerous households that are different from one another. It was about time!

This research agenda is still underway. Progress has been made on the theoretical front, but there is still controversy around the assumptions made when using the prevailing methods and their applicability to the real world. We'll see how it goes.

But some people have a different idea. They have been calling for a return to the old era of economics, taking us back to the theories that prevailed before the 1970s revolution. To them, the second era of economics is irrelevant enough to be completely ignored. This idea has been endorsed by many heterodox economists, including MMTers. We saw that in action earlier in this book—if you remember, MMT endorses Keynes' original theory of unemployment, which is 100 years old.

This idea has also been endorsed by some influential economic figures, such as Paul Krugman and Robert Skidelsky, who've been calling for a return to older, "Keynesian" economics.

I'm not sure this is a good idea. Even if mainstream economics hasn't quite done its best job yet, I have the impression that its methodological improvements have been a welcome advancement, and they may be a good canvas on which to draw the next generation of economics. Do we want to go back to the era of rules of thumb and ambiguity? Do we want to go from mathematical beauty back to mathematical ugliness? Economic historian Michel De Vroey says:

> Claiming that one should return to a theory that was proposed more than seventy years ago amounts to assuming that no progress has been made since, and that the methodological choices that offered themselves at the time are still worth considering today.[6]

Instead, I hope macroeconomics enters a new, third era, which combines methodological rigor with realism. It's not "either-or." We shouldn't have to choose between sloppy theories—such as MMT—and rigorous ones that have zero applicability to the real world.

APPENDIX A

MMT ON BITCOIN

The going prices of cryptocurrencies vary widely. Some cryptos, most notably Bitcoin, have seen their prices rise overall over time but only along a really bumpy road that never seems to flatten. Other cryptos have fallen into oblivion. This makes us wonder, what drives the value of cryptocurrencies?

MMT applies its "taxes drive money" approach to analyze cryptocurrencies. The conclusion is that cryptos don't have a credible source of value because taxes cannot be paid using them, so they have no stable, government-mandated source of value. MMTer Randall Wray explains:

> In short, the Bitcoin is an instrument used to dupe dopes ... When many people first hear MMT say that governments spend by keystrokes, they jump to the conclusion that MMT argues government doesn't need taxes. So why not just abolish them, since no one likes to pay taxes? What do you get when you drop taxes? Well, Bitcoins ... You don't need Bitcoins to make any obligatory payments. And no Bitcoin issuer is required to take them back. Bitcoins are not redeemable. Unless you are involved in illegal activity (such as the drug trade)

or trying to hide income and wealth, there's really only one compelling reason to accept them: you really do believe in the greater fool theory. You're going to dupe the dopes and ride that Bitcoin up while praying that (a) you don't lose your Bitcoin wallet, (b) your Bitcoin exchange doesn't go bankrupt, and (c) you can sell out of Bitcoins before the whole thing crashes.[1]

I'll add two observations to this. First, I think MMT is right that it's harder to find Bitcoin's source of value, compared to government money, as there are no legal obligations to use Bitcoin.

What if Bitcoin suddenly falls out of favor, perhaps because another cryptocurrency becomes trendy or people just care less about crypto in general? People have fled Facebook and gone to Instagram. Many of them then switched to TikTok. These things happen all the time. It is hard to completely flee government money because you're legally mandated to pay taxes using it, whereas it's much easier to flee a currency you don't have any legal obligation to use.

However, Bitcoin may have intrinsic value for other reasons, even if you can't pay taxes with it. So, perhaps MMT dismisses Bitcoin too quickly.

Bitcoin supporters offer different explanations of where its value comes from. One of most common ones is that Bitcoin cannot be created—by anyone—outside its initially planned schedule. This is because the ledger that says who owns how much Bitcoin, called the *blockchain*, is stored across numerous "distributed" copies around the world and thus is difficult to alter at once. So, Bitcoin is scarce, and according to its supporters, this scarcity in itself makes Bitcoin valuable.

I remain unconvinced about this. I'm not sure scarcity by itself makes anything valuable. Lots of things are scarce yet not valuable. In fact, anyone can create their own "scarce" personal cryptocurrency.

Another argument is that Bitcoin has value because one day it will be adopted as a currency commonly used for all sorts of transactions. However, Bitcoin suffers from numerous technical limitations that make it hard to use for that. For example, only a few thousand transactions can be carried out per hour, and each transaction takes a long time to settle. In addition, maintaining the record of transactions takes an enormous amount of electricity.

While MMT may dismiss Bitcoin too quickly, I haven't yet been convinced by the arguments offered by Bitcoin supporters. For that reason, I wouldn't put my life savings into Bitcoin.

APPENDIX B

MORE MMT RED HERRINGS

MMT offers numerous arguments to prove that the current, real-life United States operates just like the MMT world. According to this view, the real-life US government either already creates money on a daily basis or can do so whenever it wants to. In addition, the US government never borrows money because it absolutely must do so.

We debunked many of these arguments in Chapter 2. This appendix covers further arguments found in the MMT literature.

WHY DOES THE UNITED STATES BORROW MONEY IF IT CAN JUST CREATE IT?

Let's suppose what MMT says is true—the US government already spends money into existence, so it doesn't *need* to borrow money. However, the government keeps issuing bonds. In fact, it tends to issue $100 worth of bonds when it runs a $100 deficit. Why does it do that if borrowing is not necessary?

MMT has an interesting answer to this question. Let's go through it.

According to MMT, the government deficit floods the private sector with new money. Just do the math. Imagine the government spends $300 but collects $200 from taxes. This leaves the private sector with an extra $100, right?

We'll continue MMT's argument in a second, but let's stop here and see why this is incorrect.

Imagine I told you I can send you one million dollars via PayPal and "flood" your account with new money. You ask me to prove it. I say, "That's alright. I can do it. But can I please borrow one million dollars from you first?"

MMT forgets to count the money that flows into the government's accounts when it borrows. When the government spends $300 but only collects $200 from taxes, it borrows $100 from the private sector to top up its account and have a balance high enough to cover its spending. Three hundred dollars flows into the government—$200 from taxes and $100 from bond sales—and $300 flows out of the government when it spends. In the end, the private sector has the same amount of money it started with.

Let's continue MMT's story for the sake of argument. Let's suppose (incorrectly) that government deficits do increase the amount of money in the private sector. MMT analyzes the effect this has on commercial banks, such as HSBC. The flood of new money makes them extremely willing to extend loans, as the money in their vaults becomes plentiful. In particular, the interbank interest rate, which is the interest rate banks charge to lend money to one another, drops all the way down to zero, which means banks are happy to lend money to one another for free.[1] In addition, banks drop the interest rates they charge on mortgages, business loans, and so on. So, government deficits make it easier for everyone to borrow money, as there's more of it.

This may sound great at first, but it's bad news for the central bank. The central bank doesn't want interest rates to go too low, as it's afraid this will cause too much loan-taking and stoke inflation. So, government deficits give a massive headache to the central bank, as they flood commercial banks with too much new money and cause a drop in interest rates around the economy.

This is where bonds come to the rescue. According to MMT, the government voluntarily issues bonds to help "wipe out" the extra money that floods commercial banks due to the deficit.[2] If the government runs a $100 deficit, it sells $100 worth of bonds just to remove $100 from the likes of HSBC and prevent a drop of interest rates, which would upset the central bank. The government doesn't sell $100 in bonds to borrow money; it does so to give a helping hand to the central bank.

MMTer Randall Wray explains that the government's help is extremely effective:

> That this all operates exceedingly smoothly is evidenced by a relatively stable overnight interbank interest rate—even with rather wild fluctuations of the Treasury's budget positions.[3]

MMT's story suffers from many problems. First, deficits do *not* flood commercial banks with extra money. As explained previously, MMT forgets to count the money that goes from the private sector to the government when the latter borrows. So, deficits don't cause a permanent drop in interest rates like MMT suggests.[4]

In addition, events after the 2008 financial crisis have challenged MMT's explanation in new ways. In the aftermath of the crisis, the Fed set a very low target on the interbank rate, close to zero, in order to stimulate economic activity. The Fed didn't need to maintain a high interest rate. Nonetheless, the US Treasury kept issuing bonds that are allegedly used to help lower the interest rate. Why did it do so if such a helping hand wasn't needed anymore?

MMT proponent Éric Tymoigne provides a few answers to this. One of them is inertia—the government continued issuing bonds just because it wasn't willing to change its usual procedures. Tymoigne explains, "The Treasury needs to fund itself according to existing procedures that we have discussed in detail—procedures that can be changed or eliminated, and, indeed, are occasionally changed."[5]

As an alternative explanation, Tymoigne suggests that the Fed's interbank target was still slightly positive, not exactly zero, so the government still issued bonds to help prevent the rate from dropping all the way down to exactly zero. This is hard to believe because the Fed implemented a mechanism to guarantee a low, nonzero interbank rate.[6]

One more explanation provided by Tymoigne is that bonds are often used for all sorts of things by the public, so the government chose to issue them voluntarily after 2008 so people could rely on them. He explains that bonds are often used "to help financial institutions meet their capital requirements and to provide a foundation upon which all other securities are valued."[7] He mentions that, in the early 2000s, Australia issued bonds while running a fiscal surplus instead of a deficit. During this period, Australia didn't need to borrow to pay the bills, but it still issued bonds so that financial institutions could use them.[8]

This is all a bit hard to believe. In 2011 and 2013, the US government hit the debt ceiling imposed by Congress because it kept issuing more and more bonds and thus piling up more and more debt. This resulted in dramatic political crises and market turmoil. Why would politicians endure such crises if they could just create money instead of issuing bonds?

THE END RESULT IS THE SAME

As opposed to the private sector, the Fed is not allowed to buy government bonds directly when the government auctions them. As explained in Chapter 2, this is to preserve central bank independence. MMT responds, "Does it really matter? The end result is the same!"

MMT says that, at the very end, when you consider all operations, the result is exactly the same whether it is the central bank or a private buyer who buys a newly issued government bond. To see the truth, you just need to carefully analyze and compare these two possibilities using balance sheets, which are accounting tables.

MMTer Randall Wray explains, "With the procedures actually adopted, the transactions are more complex and the sequencing is different. But the final balance sheet position is the same."[9] MMTer Éric Tymoigne concludes that, because restrictions make no difference, "they could be dropped to simplify procedures."[10]

I was puzzled the first time I saw the balance sheets presented by MMT, as indeed the end result in both alternatives is the same.[11] But how could this be possible? How could selling a bond to the central bank—which creates money to pay for it—be the same as selling it to you, me, or a pension fund, which cannot create money to pay for it? It didn't quite add up in my mind. I then found the problem with the analysis.

I will first share an informal intuition of the problem. I'll then share the balance sheet analysis.

MMT makes an unreasonable assumption that enables it to make the balance sheets look the same in both scenarios. MMT assumes that commercial banks are always willing to purchase and hold 100% of the bonds issued by the government, and nobody else buys government bonds—ever.

Commercial banks are allowed to create money within regulatory limits (something not a lot of people are aware of). So, by making the assumption that commercial banks buy all the government bonds, MMT gives the government access to "bottomless" money created by commercial banks. This is key to making the balance sheets look the same.

There are two problems with MMT's assumption. First, commercial banks are not obliged to buy 100% of government bonds. They may buy some bonds at their own discretion if it makes economic sense to them.

Second, the assumption is at odds with reality. Data show that commercial banks only buy a minority of the bonds issued by the government.[12] Government bonds are routinely purchased by ordinary people, businesses, pension funds, and so on.

Now, let's get to the balance sheets. This is more technical, so if you're not familiar with how modern banking works, you may want to skip it.

Let's start by studying the case in which the government sells bonds directly to the central bank.

First, the central bank buys a government bond and creates new money to pay for it, which is placed in the government's account at the central bank (called TGA in the United States):

Central Bank Assets	Central Bank Liabilities	Government Assets	Government Liabilities
+ Bond	+ $100 TGA deposits	+ $100 TGA deposits	+ Bond

Afterward, the government pays a contractor, called Smith Engineering, for a job. The contractor has its account at HSBC. Here are the balance sheets after the check clears:

Central Bank Assets	Central Bank Liabilities	Government Assets	Government Liabilities
+ Bond	+ $100 HSBC reserves		+ Bond

HSBC Assets	HSBC Liabilities	Smith Engineering Assets
+ $100 reserves	+ $100 Smith Engineering's deposits	+ $100 deposits at HSBC

MMT assumes that the central bank wants to "wipe out" the excess reserves in the commercial banking system. This is to prevent a drop of the interest rate below target. So, the central bank sells the bond to a commercial bank and removes the excess reserves from the system. Here's the end result:

Central Bank Assets	Central Bank Liabilities	Government Assets	Government Liabilities
			+ Bond

HSBC Assets	HSBC Liabilities	Smith Engineering Assets
+ Bond	+ $100 Smith Engineering's deposits	+ $100 deposits at HSBC

Note that the last step is not the standard procedure followed by the central bank to alter the interest rate, as it is no longer necessary to wipe out excess reserves to hit a minimum interest rate.[13] Also, note that MMT assumes that commercial banks are always willing to buy government bonds from the central bank and that they're willing to pay the same price the central bank paid for them before. I don't think this assumption is completely innocent,[14] but let's go with it.

The last balance sheet shows that all these steps result in the creation of $100, in the form of demand deposits at commercial banks (M1 increases by $100, which is the column "HSBC liabilities").

Let's now turn to other scenario, in which the government sells the bond to the private sector instead. MMT assumes (unreasonably) that only commercial banks buy government bonds. These banks create new demand deposits to pay for them. It also assumes that commercial banks are willing to buy *all* the bonds the government intends to sell. Here's the result of such a bond purchase:

Central Bank Assets	Central Bank Liabilities	Government Assets	Government Liabilities
		+ $100 deposits at HSBC	+ Bond

HSBC Assets	HSBC Liabilities	Smith Engineering Assets
+ Bond	+ $100 Government's Deposits	

Here's what happens after the government pays the contractor:

Central Bank Assets	Central Bank Liabilities	Government Assets	Government Liabilities
			+ Bond

HSBC Assets	HSBC Liabilities	Smith Engineering Assets
+ Bond	+ $100 Smith Engineering's deposits	+ $100 deposits at HSBC

Just like MMT says, the final balance sheets are the same as in the previous scenario.

But let's now remove MMT's strong assumption about commercial banks buying all bonds. Let's suppose that a financial institution, say, Vanguard, buys the bond instead of a commercial bank. We assume, without loss of generality, that Vanguard also has its account at HSBC. Here's the end result, after the government pays the contractor:

Central Bank Assets	Central Bank Liabilities	Government Assets	Government Liabilities
			+ Bond

HSBC Assets	HSBC Liabilities	Smith Engineering Assets	Vanguard Assets
	− $100 Vanguard deposits + $100 Smith Engineering's deposits	+ $100 deposits at HSBC	− $100 deposits at HSBC + Bond

Note that the result is different from the previous one. No new money has been created (M1 remains unchanged). This shows that borrowing money from the central bank does *not* in general produce the same end result as borrowing money from the private sector, contrary to what MMT says.

THE REPO ARGUMENT

When private bond dealers buy government bonds, they sometimes borrow money temporarily from the central bank to do so. These loans, known as repurchase agreements or *repos*, are very short lived. Usually, the dealer must repay the loan within a couple of days. Repos facilitate bond buying to dealers who expect to receive funds soon but don't have them yet.

MMTers imply that repos let the government bypass current restrictions and obtain funding directly from the central bank. For example, MMTer Éric Tymoigne argues that, thanks to repos, the government can "have the Federal Reserve indirectly provide funding to the Treasury through banks ... It finances the primary [bond] dealers."[15]

MMTer Scott Fullwiler adds that, when the government conducts an auction to sell bonds, "the Fed undertakes repurchase agreement operations ... to ensure sufficient reserve balances are circulating for settlement of Treasury's auction."[16]

This argument isn't convincing. Once again, MMT forgets one part of the transaction—the loan being repaid. When a bond buyer obtains a loan from the Fed using a repo, it must give the money back to the Fed soon after. We can't say the Fed pays for the bonds or provides any funding, as it only does this temporarily.

Imagine you and I are walking down the street, and I see a pair of shoes I like displayed in a storefront window. I decide to buy them but, at the checkout counter, I realize I've forgotten my wallet. I ask you if you could pay for my shoes, and then I'll pay you back when I get home. Can we say you're paying for the shoes instead of me? Not really. You only provide temporary funds to grease the wheels of the operation.

THE ARBITRAGE ARGUMENT

Central banks around the world set a target on a primordial interest rate that widely affects the economy. In the United States, for example, the Fed sets a rate on the interbank lending rate, which is the rate at which banks lend money to one another. The Fed takes actions to intervene the interbank lending market if the rate goes above or below target. The goal of this intervention is to dampen economic fluctuations and control inflation.

The interest rate on short-term government bonds tends to be very close to the interbank rate. The reason is that investors consider them of similar risk—a bank lending money to another bank for a few days is perceived as equally risky as lending money to the government for a few days. So, market forces push the rates to a similar level. This process is known as *arbitrage*.

From this, MMT concludes that the government doesn't really have funding constraints, as it can always borrow money at a low rate, close to the Fed's target. MMTer Scott Fullwiler explains:

> While the Treasury must issue bonds in order to replenish its own account when it runs a deficit … the interest rate on these bonds is largely determined by arbitrage against the Fed's target rate. This suggests that the self-imposed constraint is not really a constraint at all.[17]

This line of argumentation doesn't hold up. The central bank's target is on the interbank lending rate. It's not on the interest rate of short-term government debt. It is conceivable that the link between the two rates could be severed if people start considering them of different risk. For example, if the government was expected to default on its debt, the interest rate on government bonds would go above the interbank rate targeted by the Fed, and the government will find it hard to borrow more money. So, we cannot say that setting a target on the interbank rate theoretically implies that the government can borrow at the same rate.

APPENDIX C
MMT ON QUANTITATIVE EASING

MTers Scott Fullwiler and Randall Wray wrote a long article discussing quantitative easing (QE).[1] The article doesn't mention MMT directly. Instead, it makes two main points about QE. First, the authors don't think QE is an effective way of providing economic stimulus as intended. This is because they think households and businesses are unlikely to be encouraged to borrow and spend more in the mid of a crisis.

Second, they think QE is undemocratic. They say:

> When the Treasury engages in lending or guarantees, its funds must be approved by Congress. The Fed does not face such a budgetary constraint—it can commit Uncle Sam to trillions of dollars of commitments without going to Congress.[2]

These two points have been raised by other economists over the years.³ For once, MMTers' views are aligned with the views of other economists.

Fullwiler and Wray do not recommend using QE for stimulus and suggest instead "a much more direct approach," which is "to target growth in after tax incomes and job creation through appropriate and sufficiently large fiscal actions." This seems to be a call for MMT-recommended policies, such as the job guarantee program.

In 2021, Stephanie Kelton wrote a blog article entitled "MMT ≠ QE."⁴ The article says that MMT was never a proposal to "print money" or to encourage central banks to engage in QE. Instead, "MMT has offered a (superior) descriptive framework, one that explains the actual mechanics of government finance." She then doubles down on MMT's long-disproven explanation of such mechanics:

> Congress never has to check the balance in its bank account to figure out whether it can afford to spend more. As the issuer of the currency, it doesn't have to worry about running out of money ... There's just no other way for it to work. It has nothing to do with QE! So please, don't conflate MMT with QE.⁵

APPENDIX D

MORE ON INFLATION

This appendix expands on two topics related to inflation. First, we discuss current inflation-fighting policies and why MMTers don't like them. We then comment on Argentina's recent disinflation.

CENTRAL BANK CRUELTY

Central banks around the world make controlling inflation one of their topmost priorities. For this, they estimate the amount of total spending in the economy that they think is compatible with low inflation. This is known as *potential spending* (or "potential output"). Unlike MMTers, central bankers do not believe in the on/off theory of inflation. So, they accept that some resources will remain unutilized in the economy when it runs at this potential level. For example, there may be some idle machines, some unemployed workers, and some unused materials.

When the central bank predicts the economy will overheat, meaning total spending will rise above potential, they try to discourage spending. They do this by raising the interest rate, hoping this will discourage spending through various channels. This is often expected to cause an increase in unemployment. The central bank is okay with it, as it believes unemployment below a certain threshold is a sign of overheating and is incompatible with low inflation.

MMTers are strongly against this procedure, and they're quite dramatic about it. MMTer Stephanie Kelton says, "To put it crudely, the Fed uses unemployed human beings as its primary weapon against inflation."[1] She then adds, "The Fed sees too much risk in letting everyone who wants to work to do so."[2]

MMTer William Mitchell adds, "Unemployment as a stabilization tool not only violates human rights, including the right to employment, it also sacrifices economic performance."[3]

My impression is that MMT interprets central bank policies in an overly unfavorable way. MMT's interpretation seems to be that central bankers are too lazy to use better tools to fight inflation, so they rely on unemployment for it. In reality, central bankers don't think inflation can be stable while at the same time unemployment is zero—they think both are incompatible. In fact, they don't think zero unemployment is even possible due to frictions and complicated job search processes in the labor market.

MMTers also think that central banks are too pessimistic in their calculations. For example, they wrongly calculate that a certain level of unemployment would cause inflation when it would not. They think this is all ideologically motivated. According to William Mitchell, there is a "neoliberal mindset that shapes the statistical representations to deliver results that reinforce the dominant ideology."[4]

Perhaps it is true that official calculations are not accurate—many people have indeed criticized them. But MMT doesn't provide a credible alternative calculation. For example, MMT says that unemployment can be zero without inflation, which most economists don't agree with.

MMT also says that, even if spending were pushed above its potential, and this caused inflation, it would not cause *accelerating* inflation. The reason is that an overheated economy may become more productive as a result of overheating. For example, if unemployment went down significantly, more workers would gain valuable experience. This would make them more productive, which would increase productive capacity and thus dampen inflationary pressure.[5] This effect, known as hysteresis, is accepted by most economists. However, most of them don't believe the effect is so strong that it will prevent acceleration of inflation if the government goes on a spending spree.

ARGENTINA'S CHAINSAW

In the height of Argentina's latest surge of inflation, presidential candidate Javier Milei rose to prominence. He said that, once elected, he'd put an end to inflation by eliminating the government deficit and stopping the practice of creating money to fund it. For this, he would severely cut down government spending.

During his campaign, Milei took a chainsaw on a stage and waved it in front of the public, signaling his commitment to cutting down the size of the government. The footage went viral in social media around the world.

Milei is a controversial figure. He holds many extravagant opinions and has bad manners. I will not be commenting on any of that. Instead, let's focus on inflation.

After Milei took office, he immediately cut government spending in a draconian way. He also stopped the practice of creating money to directly fund the government.

The inflation rate dropped 10-fold abruptly. As of this writing, the rate is still high for international standards—in the double digits—but it's noticeably lower for the local population, and it seems to be steadily going down. Or at least for now.

I'll add two comments to this. First, we'll probably hear two contrasting explanations for Argentina's disinflation. Some people—especially the supporters of Javier Milei—will say it's due to fiscal restraint and the end of money creation to fund the government. They will highlight the similarity of this experience to the 1920s disinflation in Europe, discussed in Chapter 4. Other people—especially the detractors of Javier Milei—will say disinflation is caused by recession and unemployment, which are due to shrinking the government too much, too fast. So, as with many economic questions, you'll obtain different answers depending on whom you ask. As this is an ongoing development, the jury is still out.

Second, I'm not sure lower inflation will last, as a lot of things can happen in the near future. For example, even if the recent disinflation was indeed the result of fiscal restraint, such a restraint may not be maintained. We'll see what happens.

ACKNOWLEDGMENTS

A special thank you goes to my beta readers—Eugenio, Fiodar, Heather, Ilya, Jesse, Juan, Richard, and Peter. You've offered me invaluable feedback to help me improve the manuscript.

I'd also like to thank the team at Wiley for trusting me with this project and for helping me along the way.

Thanks, everyone!

ABOUT THE AUTHOR

Emmanuel Maggiori, PhD, is a committed myth-buster. He writes books that dismantle the shiny, overhyped topic of the day, from artificial intelligence to unicorn tech start-ups. He's the author of *Smart Until It's Dumb*, *Siliconned*, and *The AI Pocket Book*.

Maggiori has a background in software engineering and did his PhD in artificial intelligence. When he's not writing or doing research for his books, he's helping technology companies build challenging software products.

NOTES

INTRODUCTION

1. An alternative, more modern explanation is that the government creates too much demand for products and services, and this increases prices. In this view, the quantity of money does not increase prices directly—increased demand (facilitated by money creation) does.
2. Robert J. Shiller, "Modern Monetary Theory Makes Sense, Up to a Point," Business, *New York Times*, March 29, 2019, https://www.nytimes.com/2019/03/29/business/modern-monetary-theory-shiller.html.
3. Liz Capo McCormick, "Jerome Powell Says the Concept of MMT Is 'Just Wrong,'" *Bloomberg.Com*, February 26, 2019, https://www.bloomberg.com/news/articles/2019-02-26/jay-powell-is-no-fan-of-mmt-says-the-concept-is-just-wrong.
4. Mervyn King, "The Ideological Bankruptcy of Modern Monetary Theory," *The Spectator*, December 17, 2020, https://www.spectator.co.uk/article/the-ideological-bankruptcy-of-modern-monetary-theory/.
5. James Mackintosh, "Modern Monetary Theory Isn't the Future. It's Here Now," *Wall Street Journal*, November 21, 2021, https://www.wsj.com/economy/central-banking/modern-monetary-theory-isnt-the-future-its-here-now-11637446538.

6. "Opinion | Modern Monetary Theory Has Never Worked," *Wall Street Journal*, July 2, 2024, https://www.wsj.com/opinion/modern-monetary-theory-has-never-worked-201759da.
7. See, e.g., Eliza Relman, "Alexandria Ocasio-Cortez Says the Theory That Deficit Spending Is Good for the Economy Should 'Absolutely' Be Part of the Conversation," *Business Insider*, accessed September 26, 2025, https://www.businessinsider.com/alexandria-ocasio-cortez-ommt-modern-monetary-theory-how-pay-for-policies-2019-1.
   See also Jordan Malter, "Bernie Sanders' 2016 Economic Advisor Stephanie Kelton on Modern Monetary Theory and the 2020 Race," *CNBC*, March 2, 2019, https://www.cnbc.com/2019/03/01/bernie-sanders-economic-advisor-stephanie-kelton-on-mmt-and-2020-race.html.
8. See, e.g., Wendy Carlin and David Soskice, *Macroeconomics: Institutions, Instability, and Inequality* (OUP, Oxford, 2023).
9. See, e.g., Satyajit Das, "Spending Without Taxing: Now We're All Guinea Pigs in an Endless Money Experiment," Opinion, *The Guardian*, December 10, 2021, https://www.theguardian.com/commentisfree/2021/dec/10/spending-without-taxing-now-were-all-guinea-pigs-in-an-endless-money-experiment.
10. Jeanna Smialek, "Is This What Winning Looks Like?" Business, *New York Times*, February 6, 2022, https://www.nytimes.com/2022/02/06/business/economy/modern-monetary-theory-stephanie-kelton.html.
11. L. Randall Wray, "The 'Kansas City' Approach to Modern Money Theory," *SSRN Electronic Journal*, ahead of print, 2020, https://doi.org/10.2139/ssrn.3650357.
12. Warren Mosler, *Soft Currency Economics*, Working paper, Macroeconomics (University Library of Munich, Germany, 1995), https://EconPapers.repec.org/RePEc:wpa:wuwpma:9502007.
13. Annie Lowrey, "Warren Mosler, a Deficit Lover With a Following," Business, *New York Times*, July 4, 2013, https://www.nytimes.com/2013/07/05/business/economy/warren-mosler-a-deficit-lover-with-a-following.html.

CHAPTER 1

1. Nick Allen, "Nicholas Cage 'Ruined by Lavish Spending on Cars, Castles and Yachts,'" *The Telegraph*, November 19, 2009, https://www.telegraph.co.uk/news/celebritynews/6599802/Nicholas-Cage-ruined-by-lavish-spending-on-cars-castles-and-yachts.html.

2. Joseph Ax, "Actor Nicolas Cage Returns Stolen Dinosaur Skull He Bought," Lifestyle, *Reuters*, December 22, 2015, https://www.reuters.com/article/lifestyle/actor-nicolas-cage-returns-stolen-dinosaur-skull-he-bought-idUSKBN0U42NQ/.
3. Emmie Martin, "How Nicolas Cage Blew $150 Million on Mansions, a Private Island—and a Real Dinosaur Skull," *CNBC*, May 10, 2017, https://www.cnbc.com/2017/05/10/craziest-things-nicholas-cage-bought-with-150-million.html.
4. "EDITORIAL: 'Raising Debt Limit Is a Sign of Failure,'" *The Washington Times*, accessed September 26, 2025, https://www.washingtontimes.com/news/2013/oct/16/editorial-raising-debt-limit-is-a-sign-of-failure/.
5. Javier Milei, Capitalismo, socialismo y la trampa neoclásica: De la teoría económica a la acción política (Planeta Argentina, 2024).
6. Stephanie Kelton, *The Deficit Myth: Modern Monetary Theory and How to Build a Better Economy*, Paperback edition (John Murray, 2021), 16.
7. Kelton, *The Deficit Myth*, 2, 13.
8. This is known as the consolidation hypothesis.
9. Dror Goldberg, "The Massachusetts Paper Money of 1690," *The Journal of Economic History* 69, no. 4 (2009): 1092–106.
10. You can see an example here: https://www.alamy.com/first-american-paper-money-colonial-massachusetts-1690-woodcut-with-image60517598.html.
11. See, e.g., L. Randall Wray, *Modern Money Theory: A Primer on Macroeconomics for Sovereign Monetary Systems*, 2nd ed. (Palgrave Macmillan, UK, 2015), https://doi.org/10.1057/9781137539922.
12. Éric Tymoigne and L. Randall Wray, *Modern Money Theory 101: A Reply to Critics*, Working Papers Series No. 778 (Levy Economics Institute, 2013), https://papers.ssrn.com/abstract=2348704, 10.
13. Hernan Nessi, "Argentina Annual Inflation Tops 211%, Highest Since Early 90s," Markets, *Reuters*, January 11, 2024, https://www.reuters.com/markets/argentina-annual-inflation-tops-211-highest-since-early-90s-2024-01-11/.
14. "Buying a Property in Argentina? Avoid These Mistakes," *TheLatinvestor*, November 22, 2023, https://thelatinvestor.com/blogs/news/argentina-property-pitfalls.
15. Wray, *Modern Money Theory: A Primer*, 52.
16. Éric Tymoigne, *Seven Replies to the Critiques of Modern Money Theory*, Working Papers Series No. 996 (Levy Economics Institute, 2021), https://papers.ssrn.com/abstract=3984305, 38.

17. Tymoigne, *Seven Replies*, 38.
18. Marc Lavoie, "Modern Monetary Theory: The Good, the Bad and the Ugly," in *Post Keynesian Economics: Key Debates and Contending Perspectives*, ed. John Curtin et al., Key Debates and Contending Perspectives Series (Edward Elgar Publishing Limited, 2024).
19. Kelton, *The Deficit Myth*, 12.
20. Kelton, *The Deficit Myth*, 33.
21. Wray, *Modern Money Theory: A Primer*, 292.
22. Kelton, *The Deficit Myth*, 11.
23. See, e.g., abstract of Tymoigne and Wray, *Modern Money Theory 101: A Reply to Critics*, https://papers.ssrn.com/abstract=2348704.
24. Thomas I. Palley, "Money, Fiscal Policy, and Interest Rates: A Critique of Modern Monetary Theory," *Review of Political Economy* 27, no. 1 (2015): 1–23, https://doi.org/10.1080/09538259.2014.957466, 4.
25. Kelton, *The Deficit Myth*, 36.
26. Kelton, *The Deficit Myth*, 36.
27. Kelton, *The Deficit Myth*, 90.
28. Kelton, *The Deficit Myth*, 87.
29. Andrew McFarland Davis, *Currency and Banking in the Province of the Massachusetts-Bay* (American Economic Association, 1901), 89.
30. Tymoigne, *Seven Replies*, 56.
31. Kelton, *The Deficit Myth*, 108, 111.
32. Kelton, *The Deficit Myth*, 116.
33. Kelton, *The Deficit Myth*, 107.
34. Wray, *Modern Money Theory: A Primer*, 292.
35. Kelton, *The Deficit Myth*, 3–4, 40.
36. See, for example, Yeva Nersisyan and L. Randall Wray, *How to Pay for the Green New Deal*, Working Papers Series No. 931 (Levy Economics Institute, 2019), https://papers.ssrn.com/abstract=3398983.
37. Kelton, *The Deficit Myth*, 56.
38. Tymoigne, *Seven Replies*, https://papers.ssrn.com/abstract=3984305.
39. Tymoigne and Wray, *Modern Money Theory 101: A Reply to Critics*, https://papers.ssrn.com/abstract=2348704, 28, 30.
40. Kelton, *The Deficit Myth*, 4.

Notes

CHAPTER 2

1. These are called Treasury Tax and Loan accounts, or TT&L accounts.
2. Brett Fiebiger, *Modern Money Theory and the "Real-World" Accounting of 1-1<0: The U.S. Treasury Does Not Spend as per a Bank*, Working Papers 279—*Modern Monetary Theory: A Debate* (Political Economy Research Institute, University of Massachusetts at Amherst, 2012), https://peri.umass.edu/publication/modern-monetary-theory-a-debate/, 1, 8, 12.
3. William Mitchell, *Deficit Spending 101—Part 2*, February 23, 2009, https://billmitchell.org/blog/?p=352.
4. Mitchell, *Deficit Spending 101—Part 2*.
5. William Mitchell and Joan Muysken, *Full Employment Abandoned: Shifting Sands and Policy Failures* (Edward Elgar, 2008), 210.
6. Kelton, *The Deficit Myth*, 29.
7. Kelton was one of the authors who replied to Brett Fiebiger's criticism, published eight years before *The Deficit Myth* came out, so she must have been aware of the issue.
8. L. Randall Wray, "Memo to Congress: Don't Increase the Government's Debt Limit!" *New Economic Perspectives*, November 19, 2009, https://neweconomicperspectives.org/2009/11/memo-to-congress-dont-increase.html.
9. Stephanie Bell, *Can Taxes and Bonds Finance Government Spending?* Working Papers Series No. 244 (Levy Economics Institute, 1998), https://papers.ssrn.com/abstract=115128, 21.
10. Fiebiger, "Real-World" Accounting, 7.
11. Scott Fullwiler et al., *Modern Money Theory: A Response to Critics*, Working Papers 279—*Modern Monetary Theory: A Debate* (Political Economy Research Institute, University of Massachusetts at Amherst, 2012), https://peri.umass.edu/publication/modern-monetary-theory-a-debate/, 17.
12. Fullwiler et al., A Response to Critics, 23.
13. Brett Fiebiger, *A Rejoinder to "Modern Money Theory: A Response to Critics,"* Working Papers 279—*Modern Monetary Theory: A Debate* (Political Economy Research Institute, University of Massachusetts at Amherst, 2012), https://peri.umass.edu/publication/modern-monetary-theory-a-debate/, 27.
14. Ryan Tate, "Meet the Genius Behind the Trillion-Dollar Coin and the Plot to Breach the Debt Ceiling," *Wired*, January 10, 2013, https://www.wired.com/2013/01/trillion-dollar-coin-inventor/.

15. Éric Tymoigne, *Modern Money Theory and Interrelations Between the Treasury and the Central Bank: The Case of the United States*, Working Papers Series No. 788 (Levy Economics Institute, 2021), https://ssrn.com/abstract=2407521, 20.
16. Edmund C. Moy, "Former U.S. Mint Director: The $1 Trillion Platinum Coin Ain't Worth a Plugged Nickel," NetNet, *CNBC*, January 8, 2013, https://www.cnbc.com/2013/01/08/former-us-mint-director-the-1-trillion-platinum-coin-aint-worth-a-plugged-nickel.html.
17. Gil Aegerter, "Treasury: No, We Won't Mint $1 Trillion Platinum Coin to Avoid Debt Ceiling," *NBC News*, January 12, 2013, http://www.nbcnews.com/politics/politics-news/treasury-no-we-wont-mint-1-trillion-platinum-coin-avoid-flna1B7952306.
18. This practice is known as debt monetization.
19. In the United States, the Fed can rollover existing debt. See "FAQs: Treasury Rollovers," *Federal Reserve Bank of New York*, accessed September 26, 2025, https://www.newyorkfed.org/markets/treasury-rollover-faq.
20. L. Randall Wray, "International Aspects of Current Monetary Policy," SSRN Scholarly Paper No. 1010156 (Social Science Research Network, 2004), https://doi.org/10.2139/ssrn.1010156, 7.
21. Wray, *Modern Money Theory: A Primer*, 105, 109.
22. See comments in Fiebiger, *"Real-World" Accounting*, https://peri.umass.edu/publication/modern-monetary-theory-a-debate/.
23. George Selgin, "On Empty Purses and MMT Rhetoric," *Cato Institute*, March 5, 2019, https://www.cato.org/blog/empty-purses-mmt-rhetoric.
24. Tymoigne, *Interrelations*, 13–14.
25. Steve Keen, *The New Economics: A Manifesto* (Polity, 2021), 43.
26. "HM Treasury and Bank of England Announce Temporary Extension to Ways and Means Facility," *Bank of England*, accessed September 26, 2025, https://www.bankofengland.co.uk/news/2020/april/hmt-and-boe-announce-temporary-extension-to-ways-and-means-facility.
27. Tymoigne, *Seven Replies*, 45.
28. Kelton, *The Deficit Myth*, 39.
29. Tymoigne, *Seven Replies*, 47.
30. William Mitchell et al., *Macroeconomics* (Macmillan International Higher Education, 2019), 321.
31. Fiebiger, *A Rejoinder*, 28.
32. Fiebiger, *"Real-World" Accounting*, 12.

33. Palley, "A Critique of Modern Monetary Theory," https://doi.org/10.1080/09538259.2014.957466, 21.
34. Matt Bruenig, "What's the Point of Modern Monetary Theory?" *People's Policy Project*, February 24, 2019, https://www.peoplespolicyproject.org/2019/02/24/whats-the-point-of-modern-monetary-theory/.
35. L. Randall Wray, "Paul Krugman Still Gets It Wrong: Modern Money Theory," *EconoMonitor*, August 16, 2011, https://web.archive.org/web/20150709155725/www.economonitor.com/lrwray/2011/08/16/paul-krugman-still-gets-it-wrong-modern-money-theory/.
36. Thomas I. Palley, The Critics of Modern Money Theory (MMT) Are Right, *IMK Working Paper 132* (IMK at the Hans Boeckler Foundation, Macroeconomic Policy Institute, 2014), https://ideas.repec.org//p/imk/wpaper/132-2014.html, 2.

CHAPTER 3

1. Olivier Blanchard and John Simon, "The Long and Large Decline in U.S. Output Volatility," *Brookings Papers on Economic Activity* 2001, no. 1 (2001): 135–64.
2. James H. Stock and Mark W. Watson, "Has the Business Cycle Changed and Why?" *NBER Macroeconomics Annual* 17 (2002): 159–218.
3. The usual mechanism is to lower the interbank interest rate. After 2008, this rate went down to almost zero, so it couldn't go any lower, yet the deflation threat persisted.
4. Michael Joyce et al., "The United Kingdom's Quantitative Easing Policy: Design, Operation and Impact," SSRN Scholarly Paper No. 1933696, Rochester, NY, September 19, 2011, https://papers.ssrn.com/abstract=1933696.
5. James Benford et al., "Quantitative Easing," SSRN Scholarly Paper No. 1420042, June 12, 2009, 97, https://papers.ssrn.com/abstract=1420042. See also Michael A. S. Joyce et al., "The Financial Market Impact of Quantitative Easing in the United Kingdom," *International Journal of Central Banking*, November 15, 2020, 141, https://www.ijcb.org/journal/ijcb11q3a5.htm.
6. James Benford et al., "Quantitative Easing," https://papers.ssrn.com/abstract=1420042.
7. See, e.g., Stephen D. King, *We Need to Talk About Inflation: 14 Urgent Lessons from the Last 2,000 Years* (Yale University Press, 2023).
8. Alternatively, they may let a bond expire without refinancing it.

9. "Speech by Governor Jefferson on the Implementation and Transmission of Monetary Policy," *Board of Governors of the Federal Reserve System*, accessed September 27, 2025, https://www.federalreserve.gov/newsevents/speech/jefferson20230327a.htm.
10. "Quantitative Easing," *Bank of England*, accessed September 27, 2025, https://www.bankofengland.co.uk/monetary-policy/quantitative-easing.
11. King, *We Need to Talk About Inflation*, 138.
12. *Quantitative Easing*, House of Lords, March 16, 2021, https://committees.parliament.uk/oralevidence/1920/html/.
13. Lyn Alden, "Quantitative Easing, MMT, and Inflation/Deflation: A Primer," *Lyn Alden*, May 3, 2020, https://www.lynalden.com/quantitative-easing-mmt-inflation/.
14. See, e.g., Christopher A. Sims, *Luncheon Address: Fiscal Policy, Monetary Policy and Central Bank Independence*, 2016, https://www.kansascityfed.org/Jackson%20Hole/documents/7040/SimsPaper_JH2016.pdf.
15. Fergal O'Brien, "BOE's Bailey Rejects QE Accusations, Slams Lords Committee," *Bloomberg.Com*, August 5, 2021, https://www.bloomberg.com/news/articles/2021-08-05/boe-s-bailey-rejects-qe-accusations-slams-lords-committee.
16. George Selgin, *The Menace of Fiscal QE* (CATO Institute, 2020), 26.
17. Jack Ewing and Jack Healy, "Cuts to Debt Rating Stir Anxiety in Europe," Business, *The New York Times*, April 27, 2010, https://www.nytimes.com/2010/04/28/business/global/28drachma.html.
18. Mario Draghi, "*Speech at Global Investment Conference*," July 26, 2012, https://www.ecb.europa.eu/press/key/date/2012/html/sp120726.en.html.
19. Francesco Canepa, "Italy Faces Debt Doubts Again as ECB Dials Back Support," European Markets, *Reuters*, December 22, 2021, https://www.reuters.com/markets/europe/italy-faces-debt-doubts-again-ecb-dials-back-support-2021-12-22/.
20. European Central Bank, "Outright Monetary Transactions, One Year On," *European Central Bank*, September 2, 2013, https://www.ecb.europa.eu/press/key/date/2013/html/sp130902.en.html.
21. European Central Bank, "Outright Monetary Transactions, One Year On," https://www.ecb.europa.eu/press/key/date/2013/html/sp130902.en.html.
22. European Central Bank, *Introductory Statement to the Press Conference (with Q&A)*, October 4, 2012, https://www.ecb.europa.eu/press/press_conference/monetary-policy-statement/2012/html/is121004.en.html.

23. King, *We Need to Talk About Inflation*, 68, 69.
24. *Quantitative Easing*, House of Lords, May 18, 2021, https://committees.parliament.uk/oralevidence/2193/html/.
25. Charlie Hutchence, "What You Need to Know About Buying Government Bonds (Gilts)," *Hargreaves Lansdown*, accessed September 27, 2025, https://www.hl.co.uk/shares/corporate-bonds-gilts/what-you-need-to-know-about-buying-government-bonds-gilts.
26. Marc Lavoie, "Modern Monetary Theory: The Good, the Bad and the Ugly," in *Post Keynesian Economics: Key Debates and Contending Perspectives*, ed. John Curtin et al., Key Debates and Contending Perspectives Series (Edward Elgar Publishing Limited, 2024).
27. Tommy Stubbington and Chris Giles, *Investors Sceptical over Bank of England's QE Programme*, January 5, 2021, https://www.ft.com/content/f92b6c67-15ef-460f-8655-e458f2fe2487.
28. House of Lords, *Economic Affairs Committee. Corrected Oral Evidence: Quantitative Easing*, May 18, 2021, https://committees.parliament.uk/oralevidence/2193/html/.
29. House of Lords, *Quantitative Easing*, https://committees.parliament.uk/oralevidence/2193/html/.
30. House of Lords, *Quantitative Easing*, https://committees.parliament.uk/oralevidence/2193/html/.
31. House of Lords, *Quantitative Easing: A Dangerous Addiction?* (House of Lords, 2021), https://committees.parliament.uk/publications/6725/documents/71894/default/.
32. "Bank of England Announces Gilt Market Operation," September 28, 2022, https://www.bankofengland.co.uk/news/2022/september/bank-of-england-announces-gilt-market-operation.
33. See, for example, Lyn Alden, "Full Steam Ahead: All Aboard Fiscal Dominance," *Lyn Alden*, January 8, 2025, https://www.lynalden.com/full-steam-ahead-all-aboard-fiscal-dominance/.
34. "Bank of England Opens New Contingent Non-Bank Lending Facility for Applications," *Bank of England*, January 28, 2025, https://www.bankofengland.co.uk/news/2025/january/boe-open-new-contingent-non-bank-lending-facility-for-applications.
35. See, e.g., "How We're Fixing the Foundations of the Country," *GOV.UK*, August 31, 2024, https://www.gov.uk/government/news/how-were-fixing-the-foundations-of-the-country.

NOTES

CHAPTER 4

1. Pamela McCourt Francescone, "Rome Hotels Hit New Record-High Prices for Pope Francis' Funeral," *Italiabsolutely*, May 6, 2025, https://italiabsolutely.com/news/hospitality/rome-hotels-hit-new-record-high-prices-for-pope-francis-funeral.
2. See, e.g., L. Randall Wray, *Understanding Modern Money: The Key to Full Employment and Price Stability*, Reprinted (Elgar, 2003), 84.
3. Palley, "A Critique of Modern Monetary Theory," 10.
4. In microeconomics, when a firm benefits from market power (a.k.a. imperfect competition), it will choose which price to charge, and it may respond to changes in demand by both changing its output volume and its prices.
5. Kelton, *The Deficit Myth*, 47.
6. Mitchell et al., *Macroeconomics*, 256, 257.
7. Wray, *Modern Money Theory: A Primer*, 199.
8. Nersisyan and Wray, *How to Pay for the Green New Deal*, 13.
9. Yeva Nersisya and L. Randall Wray, *Are We All MMTers Now? Not so Fast*, One-Pager No. 63 (Levy Economics Institute, 2020), https://www.levyinstitute.org/publications/are-we-all-mmters-now-not-so-fast.
10. Anand Giridharadas, "The Trillion-Dollar Woman," *The.Ink*, March 30, 2021, https://the.ink/p/stephaniekelton.
11. Nersisyan and Wray, *How to Pay for the Green New Deal*, 51.
12. Nersisyan and Wray, *How to Pay for the Green New Deal*, 1.
13. Thomas Palley, "What's Wrong with Modern Money Theory: Macro and Political Economic Restraints on Deficit-Financed Fiscal Policy," *Review of Keynesian Economics* 8, no. 4 (2020): 472–93, https://doi.org/10.4337/roke.2020.04.02, 483.
14. Palley, "Money, Fiscal Policy, and Interest Rates," 17–8.
15. Palley, "What's Wrong with Modern Money Theory," 479–81.
16. Palley, "A Critique of Modern Monetary Theory," 12.
17. Wray, *Understanding Modern Money*, 84.
18. Wray, *Understanding Modern Money*, 83, 84.
19. William Mitchell, "Zimbabwe for Hyperventilators 101," *William Mitchell–Modern Monetary Theory*, July 29, 2009, https://billmitchell.org/blog/?p=3773.
20. Tymoigne and Wray, *Modern Money Theory 101: A Reply to Critics*, 19. Tymoigne, *Seven Replies*, 15, 16.

21. This is known as the endogenous theory of money, which MMT endorses. It is true that the amount of money in existence in the private sector (demand deposits) responds to private demand for money. This is because loan issuance and loan repayments, among other things, create and destroy money. However, it's hard to believe a government deficit (used to fund its spending in excess of tax collection) that leads to "excess savings" will be perfectly offset by these operations, so that all that new money disappears. Some of the excess money may be "spent away" or exchanged against foreign currency, which could cause inflation.
22. Palley, *The Critics of Modern Money Theory (MMT) Are Right*, 11.
23. Tymoigne and Wray, *Modern Money Theory 101: A Reply to Critics*, 43.
24. Wray, *Modern Money Theory: A Primer*, 249–50.
25. "Frequently Asked Questions About Hedonic Quality Adjustment in the CPI," *Bureau of Labor Statistics*, accessed September 27, 2025, https://www.bls.gov/cpi/quality-adjustment/questions-and-answers.htm.
26. Mike Winters, "How Much Eggs Cost Every Year Since 1980—in One Chart," *CNBC*, March 25, 2025, https://www.cnbc.com/2025/03/25/how-much-eggs-cost-by-year.html.
27. "RPI: Ave Price—Eggs: Size 4 (55-60g), per Dozen—Office for National Statistics," accessed September 27, 2025, https://www.ons.gov.uk/economy/inflationandpriceindices/timeseries/cznu.
28. Wray, *Modern Money Theory: A Primer*, 251.
29. "12-Month Percentage Change, Consumer Price Index, Selected Categories," *Bureau of Labor Statistics*, accessed September 27, 2025, https://www.bls.gov/charts/consumer-price-index/consumer-price-index-by-category-line-chart.htm.
30. Wray, *Modern Money Theory: A Primer*, 252.
31. For the story of the big 1920s inflations, refer to Thomas J. Sargent, "The Ends of Four Big Inflations," in *Inflation: Causes and Effects*, ed. Robert E. Hall (University of Chicago Press, 1982), https://www.nbcr.org/books-and-chapters/inflation-causes-and-effects/ends-four-big-inflations.
32. Reproduced with permission from Thomas J. Sargent, "The Ends of Four Big Inflations," in *Inflation: Causes and Effects*, ed. Robert E. Hall (University of Chicago Press, 1982), 44. Copyright © 1982 by the National Bureau of Economic Research.
33. Sargent, "The Ends of Four Big Inflations," 53.
34. See Sargent, "The Ends of Four Big Inflations," 84.

35. Terrence Kairiza, "Unbundling Zimbabwe's Journey to Hyperinflation and Official Dollarization," *GRIPS Discussion Papers*, National Graduate Institute for Policy Studies, September 2009, 9–12, https://ideas.repec.org//p/ngi/dpaper/09-12.html.
36. *Fast Track Land Reform in Zimbabwe* (Human Rights Watch, 2002), https://www.hrw.org/report/2002/03/08/fast-track-land-reform-zimbabwe.
37. *Annual Report* (Reserve Bank of Zimbabwe, 2008), https://www.rbz.co.zw/documents/ar/2008AnnualReport.pdf.
38. Terrence Kairiza, "Unbundling Zimbabwe's Journey to Hyperinflation and Official Dollarization," *GRIPS Discussion Papers*, National Graduate Institute for Policy Studies, September 2009, 9–12, https://ideas.repec.org//p/ngi/dpaper/09-12.html.
39. *Annual Report* (Reserve Bank of Zimbabwe, 2008), https://www.rbz.co.zw/documents/ar/2008AnnualReport.pdf.
40. Mitchell et al., *Macroeconomics*, 346.
41. Mitchell, "Zimbabwe for Hyperventilators 101," https://billmitchell.org/blog/?p=3773.
42. Mitchell et al., *Macroeconomics*, 345.
43. Mitchell et al., *Macroeconomics*, 345.
44. Mitchell et al., *Macroeconomics*, 346.
45. Mitchell et al., *Macroeconomics*, 345, 346.
46. Tymoigne, *Seven Replies*, 54.
47. Mitchell, "Zimbabwe for Hyperventilators 101," https://billmitchell.org/blog/?p=3773.
48. Alicia Parlapiano et al., "Where $5 Trillion in Pandemic Stimulus Money Went," U.S., *New York Times*, March 11, 2022, https://www.nytimes.com/interactive/2022/03/11/us/how-covid-stimulus-money-was-spent.html.
49. Andy Powell et al., *Coronavirus Job Retention Scheme: Statistics* (2025), https://commonslibrary.parliament.uk/research-briefings/cbp-9152/.
50. See comments in Jeanna Smialek, "Is This What Winning Looks Like?" Business, *New York Times*, February 6, 2022, https://www.nytimes.com/2022/02/06/business/economy/modern-monetary-theory-stephanie-kelton.html. Link to original tweet: https://x.com/StephanieKelton/status/1240335674135511044.
51. Yeva Nersisya and L. Randall Wray, *Are We All MMTers Now? Not so Fast*, One-Pager No. 63 (Levy Economics Institute, 2020), https://www.levyinstitute.org/publications/are-we-all-mmters-now-not-so-fast.

52. Yeva Nersisya and L. Randall Wray, *COVID Relief and the Inflation Warriors*, One-Pager No. 65 (Levy Economics Institute, 2021), https://www.levyinstitute.org/publications/covid-relief-and-the-inflation-warriors/.
53. Stephanie Kelton, "How Do You Solve a Problem Like Inflation?" Substack Newsletter, *The Lens*, January 18, 2022, https://stephaniekelton.substack.com/p/how-do-you-solve-a-problem-like-inflation.
54. L. Randall Wray, *The Causes of Pandemic Inflation*, One-Pager No. 70 (Levy Economics Institute, 2022), https://www.levyinstitute.org/publications/the-causes-of-pandemic-inflation/.
55. Stephanie Kelton, "Catch Me on The Mehdi Hasan Show Later Today," Substack Newsletter, *The Lens*, June 20, 2022, https://stephaniekelton.substack.com/p/catch-me-on-the-mehdi-hasan-show.
56. Olivier J. Blanchard and Ben S. Bernanke, "What Caused the US Pandemic-Era Inflation?" Working Paper No. 31417 (National Bureau of Economic Research, June 2023), https://doi.org/10.3386/w31417.
57. King, *We Need to Talk About Inflation*, xxl, 143, 144.
58. Ed Conway, "Cost of Living: Bank of England Shares Responsibility for Crisis, Former Governor Says," *Sky News*, May 20, 2022, https://news.sky.com/story/cost-of-living-bank-of-england-shares-responsibility-for-crisis-former-governor-says-12617190.
59. "Venezuela—Inflation Rate from 1985 to 2026," *Statista*, accessed September 27, 2025, https://www.statista.com/statistics/371895/inflation-rate-in-venezuela/.
60. "Inflation Rate in Argentina from January 2018 to December 2024," *Statista*, accessed September 27, 2025, https://www.statista.com/statistics/1320016/monthly-inflation-rate-argentina/.
61. "La Presidenta Entregó La Netbook 5 Millones de Conectar Igualdad," *ANSES*, July 1, 2015, https://web.archive.org/web/20150703233943/http://www.anses.gob.ar/noticia/la-presidenta-entrego-la-netbook-millones-de-conectar-igualdad-286.
62. Rudiger Dornbusch and Sebastian Edwards, *The Macroeconomics of Populism in Latin America*, Working Papers, Macroeconomic Adjustment and Growth (World Bank, 1989), https://documents1.worldbank.org/curated/en/823061468776408577/pdf/multi0page.pdf.
63. Dornbusch and Edwards, *The Macroeconomics of Populism in Latin America*, https://documents1.worldbank.org/curated/en/823061468776408577/pdf/multi0page.pdf.
64. "Las 5 Medidas de Alberto Fernández Para Levantar La Economía," *Tiempo Argentino*, July 10, 2019, https://web.archive.org/web/20190831013933/

https://www.tiempoar.com.ar/nota/las-5-claves-de-alberto-fernandez-para-levantar-la-economia.

65. Sebastian Edwards, "Modern Monetary Theory: Cautionary Tales from Latin America," *Cato Journal* 39, no. 3 (2019): 529–61, https://doi.org/10.36009/CJ.39.3.3.
66. See the section on MMT at the end of "Lessons from the Monetary and Fiscal History of Latin America," in *A Monetary and Fiscal History of Latin America, 1960–2017*, by Carlos Esquivel et al., ed. Timothy Jerome Kehoe and Juan Pablo Nicolini (University of Minnesota Press, 2021), https://manifold.bfi.uchicago.edu/read/a-monetary-and-fiscal-history-of-latin-america-1960-2017/section/e37ca6ff-9e2d-4cfe-890d-c1f35dd14e82#ch31.
67. See concluding remarks in Rudiger Dornbusch et al., "Extreme Inflation: Dynamics and Stabilization," *Brookings Papers on Economic Activity* 1990, no. 2 (1990): 1–84, https://doi.org/10.2307/2534504.
68. See comments by Stanley Fischer, p. 65, in Rudiger Dornbusch et al., "Extreme Inflation: Dynamics and Stabilization," *Brookings Papers on Economic Activity* 1990, no. 2 (1990): 1–84, https://doi.org/10.2307/2534504.
69. Kehoe and Nicolini, eds., *A Monetary and Fiscal History of Latin America*, https://manifold.bfi.uchicago.edu/projects/monetary-fiscal-history-latin-america-1960-2017.
70. Edwards, "MMT: Cautionary Tales from Latin America," https://doi.org/10.36009/CJ.39.3.3.
71. Eric Levitz, "Real Modern Monetary Theory Has Never Been Tried," *Intelligencer*, February 8, 2022, https://nymag.com/intelligencer/2022/02/real-modern-monetary-theory-has-never-been-tried.html.
72. High inflation tends to also be more volatile. So, the higher the inflation, the higher to predict the actual inflation rate.
73. Filipe R. Campante et al., *Advanced Macroeconomics: An Easy Guide* (LSE Press, 2021), 313.
74. Campante et al., *Advanced Macroeconomics*, 312–13.
75. "Inflation and the 2% Target," accessed September 27, 2025, https://www.bankofengland.co.uk/monetary-policy/inflation.
76. Jeanna Smialek, "Is This What Winning Looks Like?" Business, *New York Times*, February 6, 2022, https://www.nytimes.com/2022/02/06/business/economy/modern-monetary-theory-stephanie-kelton.html.
77. Mitchell et al., *Macroeconomics*.
78. See, e.g., Campante et al., *Advanced Macroeconomics*.

79. Wray, *Modern Money Theory: A Primer*, 253.
80. See, e.g., Javier Andrés and Ignacio Hernando, "Does Inflation Harm Economic Growth? Evidence for the OECD," SSRN Scholarly Paper No. 226472, Rochester, NY, June 1, 1997, https://papers.ssrn.com/abstract=226472.
81. See comments by Otmar Issing in Kunio Okina et al., "Concluding Panel Discussion: Sustained Economic Growth and Central Banking," *Monetary and Economic Studies, Institute for Monetary and Economic Studies, Bank of Japan* 22, no. S1 (2004): 217–48.
82. Kelton, *The Deficit Myth*, 54.

CHAPTER 5

1. See, e.g., Campante et al., *Advanced Macroeconomics*.
2. You can find an explanation of this process in Mitchell et al., *Macroeconomics*, 196.
3. Henry Hazlitt, *The Failure of the "New Economics": An Analysis of the Keynesian Fallacies* (D. Van Nostrand Company, 1967), 47, 105.
4. Mitchell et al., *Macroeconomics*, 196.
5. MMTers may respond by alluding to the "fallacy of composition," which is when we wrongly extrapolate individual behavior to the global behavior of the group. But I don't think it applies here. It is hard to imagine that the "community" of entrepreneurs will think, "more employment leads to more sales," when no entrepreneur does this individually.
6. Mitchell et al., *Macroeconomics*, 196.
7. Mitchell et al., *Macroeconomics*, 199.
8. For a discussion on this confusion, see De Vroey, *Involuntary Unemployment*.
9. De Vroey, *Involuntary Unemployment*, 80.
10. John Maynard Keynes, *The General Theory of Employment, Interest, and Money: The Economic Consequences of the Peace*, Wordsworth Classics of World Literature (Wordsworth, 2017), 28.
11. Axel Leijonhufvud, "Did Keynes Mean Anything? Rejoinder to Yeager," *Cato Journal* 8, no. 1 (1988): 209–17.
12. Keynes, *The General Theory*, 224.
13. Keynes, *The General Theory*, 229.
14. See De Vroey, *Involuntary Unemployment*, 80.
15. Mitchell et al., *Macroeconomics*, 211.

16. Keynes, *The General Theory*, preface.
17. See discussion in De Vroey, *Involuntary Unemployment*, 60.
18. Most textbooks discuss Keynesian economics as the economics of "sticky prices and wages," and they use the IS/LM model to analyze it, which was developed later. The original "theory of effective demand" isn't usually mentioned.
19. Kelton, *The Deficit Myth*, 64.
20. Tymoigne, *Seven Replies,* https://papers.ssrn.com/abstract=3984305, 23.
21. Kelton, *The Deficit Myth*, 66.
22. Tymoigne, *Seven Replies,* https://papers.ssrn.com/abstract=3984305, 33.
23. Tymoigne and Wray, *Modern Money Theory 101: A Reply to Critics*, https://papers.ssrn.com/abstract=2348704, 46.
24. L. Randall Wray et al., *Public Service Employment: A Path to Full Employment*, Research Project Report (Levy Economics Institute, 2018), https://www.levyinstitute.org/publications/public-service-employment-a-path-to-full-employment, 35.
25. Tymoigne, *Seven Replies,* https://papers.ssrn.com/abstract=3984305, 34.
26. Wray et al., *Public Service Employment*, https://www.levyinstitute.org/publications/public-service-employment-a-path-to-full-employment, 8.
27. Mitchell et al., *Macroeconomics*, 304.
28. See the three categories in Wray et al., *Public Service Employment*, https://www.levyinstitute.org/publications/public-service-employment-a-path-to-full-employment, 24.
29. Mitchell et al., *Macroeconomics*, 304.
30. See Wray, *Understanding Modern Money*, 134.
31. Wray, *Understanding Modern Money*, 135.
32. Tymoigne and Wray, *Modern Money Theory 101: A Reply to Critics*, https://papers.ssrn.com/abstract=2348704, 46–7. Tymoigne, *Seven Replies,* https://papers.ssrn.com/abstract=3984305, 28.
33. Mitchell et al., *Macroeconomics*, 304.
34. Robert P. Murphy, *Understanding Money Mechanics* (Mises Institute, 2021), 203.
35. Tymoigne, *Seven Replies,* https://papers.ssrn.com/abstract=3984305, 34.
36. Wray, *Understanding Modern Money*, 130.
37. Wray et al., *Public Service Employment*, https://www.levyinstitute.org/publications/public-service-employment-a-path-to-full-employment, 2.
38. Malcolm Sawyer, "Employer of Last Resort: Could It Deliver Full Employment and Price Stability?" *Journal of Economic Issues* 37, no. 4 (2003): 881–907.

39. Sawyer, "Employer of Last Resort."
40. Sawyer, "Employer of Last Resort."
41. Palley, "A Critique of Modern Monetary Theory," https://doi.org/10.1080/09538259.2014.957466, 20.
42. Palley, *The Critics of Modern Money Theory (MMT) Are Right*, https://ideas.repec.org///imk/wpaper/132-2014.html, 19.
43. E.g., political challenges are not mentioned in the MMT textbook, Mitchell et al., *Macroeconomics*.
44. Tymoigne, *Seven Replies*, https://papers.ssrn.com/abstract=3984305, 33.
45. Tymoigne, *Seven Replies*, https://papers.ssrn.com/abstract=3984305, 33.
46. See, e.g., Wray, *Modern Money Theory: A Primer*, https://doi.org/10.1057/9781137539922, 237.
47. Irene Bucci and Laura Bucci, "El Plan Jefes y Jefas de Hogar-Asistencialismo, Precarización y Segmentación Laboral Según Género," Paper Presented at IV Jornadas de Sociología de la UNLP, November 23, 2005, https://www.memoria.fahce.unlp.edu.ar/trab_eventos/ev.6614/ev.6614.pdf, 5. See also *Plan Jefes y Jefas ¿Derecho Social o Beneficio Sin Derechos?* (Centro de Estudios Legales y Sociales, 2003), https://www.cels.org.ar/common/documentos/analisis_jefes_jefas_oct2003.pdf, 35.
48. Cristian Módolo, "Los Peligros Institucionales Del Plan Jefes y Jefas de Hogar," paper presented at Novenas Jornadas "Investigaciones en la Facultad" de Ciencias Económicas y Estadística, Universidad de Rosario, November 2004, https://rephip.unr.edu.ar/server/api/core/bitstreams/2eb2c7aa-fce4-4f1f-ba78-f1d544db4905/content; see page 15 of PDF, "El Ministerio de Trabajo evaluó el perfil de los beneficiarios del Plan Jefes de Hogar," Argentina.gob.ar, January 15, 2003, https://www.argentina.gob.ar/noticias/el-ministerio-de-trabajo-evaluo-el-perfil-de-los-beneficiarios-del-plan-jefes-de-hogar.
49. *Programa Familias Por La Inclusión Social:Entre El Discurso de Derechos y La Práctica Asistencial*, COLECCIÓN INVESTIGACIÓN Y ANÁLISIS N4 (Centro de Estudios Legales y Sociales, 2007), https://www.cels.org.ar/common/documentos/analisis_jefes_jefas_oct2003.pdf.
50. See, e.g., the discussion in Hunter Lewis, *Where Keynes Went Wrong: And Why World Governments Keep Creating Inflation, Bubbles, and Busts* (Axios Press, 2011), 11.

NOTES

CHAPTER 6

1. Nersisyan and Wray, *How to Pay for the Green New Deal*, 4–5. The acronym "GND" will be rewritten as "Green New Deal" for consistency throughout this chapter.
2. Congress.gov. "H.Res.109 – 116th Congress (2019–2020): Recognizing the Duty of the Federal Government to Create a Green New Deal." February 12, 2019. https://www.congress.gov/bill/116th-congress/house-resolution/109.
3. Nersisyan and Wray, *How to Pay for the Green New Deal*, https://papers.ssrn.com/abstract=3398983.
4. Nersisyan and Wray, *How to Pay for the Green New Deal*, 15.
5. Nersisyan and Wray, *How to Pay for the Green New Deal*, 19–20.
6. Nersisyan and Wray, *How to Pay for the Green New Deal*, 38.
7. I'm converting percentage of GDP to dollars from the original paper, in order to make the exposition more consistent.
8. Nersisyan and Wray, *How to Pay for the Green New Deal*, 51.
9. See, e.g., "Understanding Differences in Health Expenditure Between the United States and OECD Countries," *OECD*, September 19, 2022, https://www.oecd.org/en/publications/understanding-differences-in-health-expenditure-between-the-united-states-and-oecd-countries_6f24c128-en.html.
10. Shem Best, "INSIDE STORY: How El Salvador Dollarized," *Caribbean Progress Studies Institute*, February 9, 2024, https://cpsi.media/p/inside-story-how-el-salvador-dollarized.
11. Best, "How El Salvador Dollarized." https://cpsi.media/p/inside-story-how-el-salvador-dollarized.
12. Best, "How El Salvador Dollarized." https://cpsi.media/p/inside-story-how-el-salvador-dollarized.
13. Best, "How El Salvador Dollarized." https://cpsi.media/p/inside-story-how-el-salvador-dollarized.
14. Bitcoin was made legal tender in 2021. However, its adoption was lukewarm, probably due to its high volatility. In addition, reliance on Bitcoin made it hard for El Salvador to obtain a loan from the International Monetary Fund, so the country backtracked on its Bitcoin policy in 2024. See Santiago Pérez, "El Salvador Made Bitcoin an Official Currency. Now It's Backtracking for IMF Loan," World, *Wall Street Journal*, December 18, 2024, https://www.wsj.com/world/americas/el-salvador-made-bitcoin-an-official-currency-now-its-backtracking-for-imf-loan-874c6623.

15. Ecuador issued a limited number of coins between 2001 and 2003 to make petty transactions more convenient. The central bank issued more coins in 2023 after the original ones deteriorated. See Mónica Orozco, "Estas Son Las Nuevas Monedas Fraccionarias En Ecuador," Economía, *Primicias*, December 18, 2023, https://www.primicias.ec/noticias/economia/nuevas-monedas-bce-ecuador/.
16. Scott Squires et al., "Argentina's Milei Vows to Pay Country's Debt While Shuttering the Central Bank," *Bloomberg.Com*, August 16, 2023, https://www.bloomberg.com/news/articles/2023-08-16/milei-vows-to-pay-argentina-s-debt-while-shuttering-central-bank.
17. "The Euro: The Birth of a New Currency," European Central Bank, May 21, 1999, https://www.ecb.europa.eu/press/key/date/1999/html/sp990521.en.html.
18. Wray, *Modern Money Theory: A Primer*, 42–3, 191.
19. Wray, *Modern Money Theory: A Primer*, 190.
20. Mitchell et al., *Macroeconomics*, 518.
21. Mitchell et al., *Macroeconomics*, 518.
22. Saifedean Ammous, *The Bitcoin Standard: The Decentralized Alternative to Central Banking* (Wiley, 2021), 44.
23. Tymoigne, *Seven Replies*, 62–3.
24. Tymoigne, *Seven Replies*, 63.
25. Palley, *The Critics of Modern Money Theory (MMT) Are Right*, 17.
26. See Emmanuel Maggiori, Siliconned: How the Tech Industry Solves Fake Problems, Hoards Idle Workers, and Makes Doomed Bets with Other People's Money (2024).
27. Palley, "A Critique of Modern Monetary Theory," 18.
28. See, e.g., Jeremy B. Rudd, *A Practical Guide to Macroeconomics* (Cambridge University Press, 2024), https://doi.org/10.1017/9781009465779.
29. See, e.g., Daron Acemoglu et al., "*Institutions as the Fundamental Cause of Long-Run Growth*," Working Paper No. 10481, Working Paper Series (National Bureau of Economic Research, May 2004), https://doi.org/10.3386/w10481.
30. See Mitchell et al., *Macroeconomics*, 524.
31. Mitchell et al., *Macroeconomics*, 524.
32. Tymoigne, *Seven Replies*, 61.
33. Tymoigne, *Seven Replies*, 62.
34. This phenomenon is called hysteresis or path-dependence (high unemployment in the present can cause higher unemployment in the future).
35. MMTers may argue that higher employment arising from a job guarantee may indirectly increase productivity. For example, workers may consume more

thanks to their job guarantee wages, which may encourage factories to invest more in productivity enhancement tasks to satisfy increased demand. But this is a long shot.

CONCLUDING REMARKS: MMT AND THE FUTURE OF ECONOMICS

1. The distinction into these two phases is borrowed from De Vroey, *A History of Macroeconomics*.
2. De Vroey, *A History of Macroeconomics*, 145, 163, 167.
3. De Vroey, *A History of Macroeconomics*, 373.
4. De Vroey, *A History of Macroeconomics*, 306.
5. Rudd, *A Practical Guide to Macroeconomics*, xv, xvi.
6. De Vroey, *A History of Macroeconomics*, 388.

APPENDIX A

1. Wray, *Modern Money Theory: A Primer*, 81, 137, 139.

APPENDIX B

1. See Bell, *Can Taxes and Bonds Finance Government Spending?* 22.
2. Tymoigne and Wray, *Modern Money Theory 101: A Reply to Critics*, 26.
3. Wray, *International Aspects of Current Monetary Policy* 7.
4. There might be temporary disruptions to the interbank rate. To prevent that, until 2009, the Treasury strived to always end the day with five billion dollars in the TGA. If necessary, it would move money between this account and accounts at commercial banks to make that happen. Cash analysts met every morning at 9 a.m. to analyze the day's cashflows and plan the necessary transfers. See Paul J. Santoro, *The Evolution of Treasury Cash Management During*

the Financial Crisis, Current Issues in Economics and Finance (Federal Reserve Bank of New York, 2012), https://www.newyorkfed.org/research/current_issues/ci18-3.html.
5. Tymoigne and Wray, *Modern Money Theory 101: A Reply to Critics*, 36.
6. The Fed started paying interest on reserves, which sets a minimum baseline on the interbank rate.
7. Tymoigne and Wray, *Modern Money Theory 101: A Reply to Critics*, 32.
8. Tymoigne and Wray, *Modern Money Theory 101: A Reply to Critics*, 33.
9. Wray, *Modern Money Theory: A Primer*, 99–100.
10. Tymoigne and Wray, *Modern Money Theory 101: A Reply to Critics*, 30.
11. Compare tables in pages 321 and 339 of Mitchell et al., *Macroeconomics*. Also see tables 1 and 2 in Marc Lavoie, "The Monetary and Fiscal Nexus of Neo-Chartalism: A Friendly Critique," *Journal of Economic Issues* 47, no. 1 (2013): 1–32, https://doi.org/10.2753/JEI0021-3624470101.
12. See Brett Fiebiger, *"Real-World" Accounting*, 9.
13. The central bank pays interest on excess reserves, which sets a floor on the interbank lending rate without having to "wipe out" the reserves.
14. The implication is that government bonds are risk-free. As discussed in Chapter 3, if government bonds are truly risk-free, this means the central bank is ready to create as much money as needed to bail out the government if necessary. But this is the same as assuming that the MMT model applies already, as all central bank independence is eliminated. So, this step in the balance sheet analysis enforces "the MMT world" by assumption.
15. Tymoigne, *Interrelations*, 12, 15.
16. Scott Fullwiler et al., *A Response to Critics*, 6.
17. Scott Fullwiler et al., *A Response to Critics*, https://peri.umass.edu/publication/modern-monetary-theory-a-debate/.

APPENDIX C

1. Scott Fullwiler and L. Randall Wray, *Quantitative Easing and Proposals for Reform of Monetary Policy Operations*, Working Papers Series No. 645 (Levy Economics Institute, 2021), https://ssrn.com/abstract=1730744.
2. Fullwiler and Randall Wray, *Quantitative Easing*, 20.
3. See, e.g., Selgin, *The Menace of Fiscal QE*.

NOTES

4. Stephanie Kelton, "MMT ≠ QE," Substack Newsletter, *The Lens*, August 26, 2021, https://stephaniekelton.substack.com/p/mmt-qe.
5. Fullwiler and Randall Wray, *Quantitative Easing*, 10.

APPENDIX D

1. Kelton, *The Deficit Myth*, 52.
2. Kelton, *The Deficit Myth*, 56.
3. Mitchell et al., *Macroeconomics*, 292.
4. William Mitchell, "The NAIRU/Output Gap Scam Reprise," *Modern Monetary Theory*, February 27, 2019, https://billmitchell.org/blog/?p=41690.
5. Mitchell et al., *Macroeconomics*, 283–84.

INDEX

A
accelerating inflation, 183
animal spirits, 118, 126, 130
arbitrage argument, 176–177
Argentina's chainsaw, 114, 183–184

B
Bank of England, 3, 20, 63, 64, 71, 74, 75, 111
Baumol effect, 94
bills, 21
Bitcoin, 39, 143, 146, 155, 163–165
blockchain, 164
bullion coins, 50

C
CARES Act, 104
central bank digital currency, 44
"chainsaw" policy, 114, 183–184
ChatGPT, 86
cigarette taxes, 28
connected equality, 107
consumer price index (CPI), 93

cost-push inflation, 127
COVID-19 pandemic, 4, 55, 62, 65, 73, 75, 103
CPI. *see* consumer price index (CPI)
cryptocurrencies, 39, 146, 163, 164

D
debt, 30–31
　national, 30
　pay off, 32–33
The Deficit Myth (Kelton), 3, 10, 46
deflation, 61, 68–69, 128
Department of Government Efficiency (DOGE), 37
digital money, 22, 50
DOGE. *see* Department of Government Efficiency (DOGE)
domestic policy space, 144

E
economic growth, 149–152
economic theory, 57, 152, 159

INDEX

European Central Bank, 70, 71, 143, 144
European debt crisis, 69
exchange controls, 80
explosion of money, 89–92

F
Facebook, 164
fiat currency, 19
final balance sheets, 174
Financial Times article, 74
fiscal policy, 144
floating exchange rate, 19
full employment, 119–121, 123

G
The General Theory of Employment, Interest, and Money (Keynes), 117
government
  borrowing money, 52
  checks never bounce, 53–54
  debt, 30–31
  deficits, 33–35
  emergencies, 54–55
  households, 14
  limits, 36–37
  new money, creating, 7, 154
  not bouncing, 53–54
  pay off tomorrow, 32–33
  policy leading to theory, 154
  restrictions on spending, 7–8, 154–155
  risk-free bonds, 71–73
  run out of money, 5–6, 28–30, 153–154
  self-flagellation, 37–40
government bond, 30
Great Depression, 61, 117, 157
Green New Deal, 135–141, 144, 146

H
Hargreaves Lansdown, 72
HSBC liabilities, 174
hyperinflation, 95–102, 143
hyperventilation, 95–102, 113
hysteresis, 183

I
infamous mini-budget, 76–77
inflation
  accelerating, 183
  central bank cruelty, 181–183
  challenge, 126–130
  cost-push, 127
  COVID-19 experiment, 102–106
  exchange controls, 80
  explosion of money, 89–92
  fear of, 112, 140
  generating, 62–65
  hyperinflation, 95–102, 143
  hyperventilation, 95–102
  Latin American experiment, 106–110
  on/off switch, 81–84
  political problems, 110–113

Index

prices, 92–95
surge of, 143
tax, 111, 145
threat of, 128–129, 143
unemployment, 84–88
inflation-fighting policies, 181–184
Instagram, 164
international investors, 107
invisible money problem, 44–49
involuntary unemployment, 118, 157

J
Jefes program, 131, 132
job guarantee, 117, 125–126

K
"Keynesian" economics, 160
Keynes' theory of unemployment, 121, 128

L
Latin American experiment, 106–110
Levy Economics Institute, 9

M
macroeconomics, 112
maximum possible resource utilization, 120, 121
medium of exchange, 25
mini-budget, 76–77
Modern Monetary Theory (MMT), 3
Bitcoin, 163–165
borrow money, 168–171
challenges, 8
conditions of, 19–20
essence of, 16–19
fiat currency, 19
final balance sheets, 174
floating exchange rate, 19
future of economics, 156–161
learning from, 155–156
monetarily sovereign, 19
people of, 8–9
physical sense, 56
principles, 5–8
quantitative easing (QE), 68–69, 179–180
red herrings, 167–177
taxes drive money approach, 163
unemployment, 84–88
monetary aggregate, 47
monetary sovereignty, 19, 141–147
money printing, 89

N
national debt, 30
neoliberal politicians, 131
New York Times, 3, 4, 15
Nicolas Cage-style situations, 20

O
OECD. *see* Organisation for Economic Co-operation and Development (OECD)
OMT. *see* Outright Monetary Transactions (OMT)

on/off switch, 81–84
Organisation for Economic Co-operation and Development (OECD), 113
Outright Monetary Transactions (OMT), 70

P
PayPal, 44, 46
PCE index. *see* popular price index (PCE index)
planet and prosperity
  annihilation, 135
  economic growth, 149–152
  the Green New Deal, 136–141
  monetary sovereignty, 141–147
  zero interest rate, 147–149
policy analyst, 58
popular price index (PCE index), 94
potential spending, 181
price controls, 80

Q
QE. *see* quantitative easing (QE)
quantitative easing (QE), 4, 14
  European countries, 69–71
  generate inflation, 62–65
  mini-budget, 76–77
  MMT and, 68–69, 179–180
  overview, 61–62
  risk-free, 71–73
  strange omission, 65–67
  suspicious coordination, 73–76
quantitative tightening, 65

R
repo argument, 175–176
repurchase agreements, 175
risk-free bonds, 71–73

S
Second War Powers Act, 55
self-flagellation, 37–40
self-imposed restrictions, 6
sovereign currency, 143
special theory of relativity, 158
The Spectator (King), 3

T
tax
  abatements, 28
  drive money approach, 21–23
  enough though, 23–26
  to fight inflation, 27–28
  inflation, 111, 145
  for redistribution of income, 27
  roles of, 27–28
TGA. *see* Treasury General Account (TGA)
theory of relativity, 158
TikTok, 164
Toyota Hilux, 24

Treasury General Account (TGA), 43–44
trillion-dollar coin, 49–51

U
unemployment, 84–85, 87–88
  as chronic disease, 124
  enough jobs, 117–122
  full, 119–121, 123
  inflation challenge, 126–130
  involuntary, 118, 157
  job guarantee program, 125–126
  Keynes' theory of, 121, 128
  MMT's flagship policy, 117
  political challenge, 130–132
  reasons for, 89, 116
  wages, 122–124
  zero, 121, 182
United States, borrow money, 168–171

unit of account, 25
US federal government, 43
US Mint, 49–50

W
wage-price spiral, 127
wages, 122–124
The Wall Street Journal, 3

X
X-date, 15

Z
zero interest rate, 147–149
zero interest-rate policy (ZIRP), 148, 149
zero unemployment, 121, 182
Zimbabwean dollar, 99
ZIRP. *see* zero interest-rate policy (ZIRP)